TOURISM ECOSYSTEMS
SUSTAINABILITY MANAGEMENT AND DIGITALIZATION

MARIANGELA FRANCH   LUISA MICH   ROBERTO PERETTA

EDITORS

intra

University Series

Cover
Rota Vicentina, Portugal, Fishermen's Trail - 4th steps - Ph. ©Luisa Mich

Editors
Mariangela Franch - https://webapps.unitn.it/du/it/Persona/PER0004292
Luisa Mich - https://webapps.unitn.it/du/it/Persona/PER0001016
Roberto Peretta - https://kiwimilano.it

ISBN 979-12-5991-452-1

Table of contents

Introduction

A tourist destination is a system of complex dynamic relations between diverse actors. This system is made up of physical elements – tourist attractions and tourism operators – and of closely interlinked digital infrastructure and applications which require new management methods. The nature of the relations is such that changes in one component spread throughout the whole system. This is why the book proposes turning to network theory (which is part of complex systems theory) to describe the existing type of governance of tourism ecosystems, the different levels upon which the systems operate, and the measures to predict their evolution.

Tourist destinations, in fact, epitomise ecosystems which, on the one hand, are robust and very capable of self-organising in the face of crisis but, on the other, are rather fragile when changes directly impact their main hubs. Managing these relational systems requires the kind of flexible governance which allows stakeholder networks to participate in decision making and is able to respond rapidly to change, quickly finding new equilibria.

One of the most disruptive situations currently faced by some destinations is overtourism, a relatively new – and all too often trivialised and over-simplified – phenomenon that can only be tackled by restricting tourist numbers (presence and movement) so that they do not exceed the destination's carrying capacity. This requires a resilient problem-solving approach. Participatory governance at the appropriate level – e.g., local, regional – generally makes it much easier to implement tourist flow control, most effectively achieved by applying information systems which enable the collection and elaboration of data on spatial, temporal, structural and communication flows which can be monitored and managed.

The availability of online and offline data together with newly developed artificial intelligence technologies, the internet of things and action-tracking, web reputation monitoring, smart city projects and gamification enable policy makers and other stakeholders to develop shared strategies to effectively address the problems of maintaining equilibrium in tourism ecosystems.

A sustainable approach to destination management, supported by digital technologies, is vital if we are to reconcile short and medium term perspectives, the desire for profit with the need for resilience, tourism's negative and positive externalities, and in turn, to protect natural and cultural resources from the seemingly insatiable greed of overtourism.

This book, which combines theoretical analysis of crucial questions in the field with a rich body of real life examples, includes revised versions of the main chapters of a book published in Italian (Turismo, fragilità, emergenze, M. Franch, R. Peretta (eds.), McGraw-Hill, Milano, 2020).

Chapter 1 - Fragility and Equilibrium

Sergio Cagol - https://www.sergiocagol.it
and Mariangela Franch - https://webapps.unitn.it/du/it/Persona/PER0004292

1.1 The fragility of tourism

The analysis of tourism destinations affected by over tourism brings a central theme vividly to the fore: the fragility of the overall tourism system and the difficulty of finding solutions to the various imbalances afflicting it today.

Tourism destination

The definition of tourism destination evokes a difference between **manager-oriented approaches and customer-oriented approaches.** A destination can equally be understood as a network of suppliers, or as well as a network of suppliers activated by visitors' demands. From a geography-oriented vision, destinations are traditionally regarded as defined geographical areas, such as country, island, or town. Following this way, destinations are places toward which people travel and where they choose to stay for a while to experience certain attractions.

From a **managerial perspective**, destinations are agglomerations of facilities and services designed to meet the needs of tourists. The destination could be described as a **tourism product** that denotes a complex consumptive experience resulting from the process where tourists use multiple travel services such as information, transportation, and accommodation during their visit. The **customer-oriented** approaches referees to the experience of the tourist as activator of the destination itself.

In our perspective the destination has to be considered not a fixed and completed entity, but **a process** devoted to optimizing the relationship between producers and customers strictly intertwined in the context of the destinations. This definition takes into account the **poly-vocal issues** of tourism destination, the complex relationships between producers, consumers, local people, and authorities and the symbolic co-creation of tourist experiences based on sign value.

The causes are many, among the first the sheer complexity of the tourism ecosystem, populated by numerous private and public stakeholders who are all pursuing goals and interests which quite often diverge. This ecosystem is often unstructured, particularly when it is dominated by small and medium enterprises, and not all actors perceive the value of "systems-building". When there are extreme power imbalances, the interests of global actors – online marketing platforms, airlines, etc – often take precedence over and obscure the needs of local operators; the former follow their own business models, generating flows of people at the global level which are very hard to regulate locally (e.g., when attempts are being made to avoid over tourism).

The push towards unlimited growth generates constantly changing, asymmetric dynamics, creating the conditions for, and resulting in, an unsustainable tourism model.

1.2 Overtourism and the pandemic

While the abovementioned factors are the main causes of over tourism, in 2020 another disaster – at the other end of the spectrum – struck tourism: "no flows" of people, as the world ground to a halt in the face of Covid-19. The two phenomena – overtourism and Covid-19 – can be understood as acute expressions of the fragility of an ecosystem within which many of the actors were not (or did not wish to be) aware that there were limits to the use of natural resources, beyond which tipping points are reached which are extremely difficult, or indeed impossible, to reverse.

It is possible to deal with today's economic problems by examining the entire tourism chain and introducing a sustainable economic model into the debate, a model which allows the actors within the ecosystem to restore its equilibrium through due consideration of the social, environmental, and economic impacts of their activities. The four concepts upon which this rethinking of the model is based are: fragility, resilience, crisis (used as synonymous of emergency), and sustainability.

The term fragility indicates the predisposition to impairment of (an organism or system's) integrity, a predisposition to the possibility of damage. If we consider these themes in the tourism context, fragility is to be understood as experiencing problems when attempting to deal with critical issues, manage risk, and minimise risk factors. It also connotes an inability to develop alternative models, which allow new solutions to emerge.

Fragility, tourism, environment, and research

Until now, the world of research has addressed the concepts of "fragility" and "tourism" primarily in environmental terms, studying the damage that the arrival of tourists has caused in natural ecosystems in uninhabited territories and de-veloping countries. Many studies evoke the concept of responsible tourism, which encourages well-off, educated tourists to visit less economically devel-oped countries with different cultures and, while holidaying, to be environmen-tally responsible, with the help (and guidance) of local tour operators who have assumed the same responsibility. A smaller number of studies relate the issue of fragility to general questions of tourism governance such as overtourism and epidemics. Among these are studies from African universities, produced in geo-graphical and cultural contexts where armed conflicts, phenomena like the Ebo-la epidemic and sudden flows of large numbers of foreign visitors have caused repeated catastrophes. Zhou Zibanai at the Midlands State University in Gweru, Zimbabwe has written a literature review on this subject.

1.3 Emergency and resilience

In ecology and biology, the term **resilience** refers to the capacity of a living substance or life form to repair itself when it has been damaged and, in sociology, to the capacity of a community or ecological system to reestablish its **equilibrium** after that state has been in some way disturbed. In tourism, the most resilient areas are those where territorial and tourism systems naturally form an integrated whole, in which a diverse range of small businesses, spread throughout the territory, cooperate, and coevolve dynamically and flexibly. A territorial system's capacity to be resilient thus requires that diverse actors are willing to support each other in a joint effort to "remedy" the damage done by a perturbation, and are able to respond swiftly and appropriately in a context in which there are fewer structural restrictions than there are in bigger and consequently more rigid systems. While fragility indicates an inability to withstand certain stresses that inevitably leads to a tipping point, resilience allows an organism/system to adapt to change without losing its own primary characteristics. The first key for managing fragility in the tourism system is therefore to recognise resilience as the capacity to adapt in order to recover. There are, however, conditions in which fragility gives rise to critical situations in which resilience alone is not enough to cope with change. In the first, deeply shocking, weeks of the Covid-19 pandemic, fragility resulted in "emergency": the word on everyone's lips – from politicians to public health officials to the general public – and a constant in the media across the world.

> **Emergence**
>
> According to the Italian dictionary Treccani, emergence is also, "in botany, a protuberance from the surface of the trunk or leaves or homologous organs (that has diverse forms and functions depending on the species), that can originate not only from the epidermis but also from the underlying tissues, such as, for example, the thorns of a rose.

The word emergency is used to refer to a situation, which is completely unexpected, a critical moment, which requires immediate action, in order to tackle a public danger. Of course, it would be absurd to downplay the emergency understood in this sense, or the effects that it has had on human lives, economies worldwide, tensions between nation states and within the European Union. The word "emergence" – word with the same root as emergency – is closely related to the rise of a plant from the soil, or of archaeological, artistic, or botanical/geological etc finds from obscurity or the unknown. The ideas discussed in this book give us a sense of the very real possibility that a new economic and social model might be inspired by sustainable tourism management. In botany, new plant growth emerges not simply from the epidermis but from the underlying tissues.

If we take the epidermis as a metaphor for the "business as usual" model that has produced globalization and overtourism, we can hypothesise that one of (and the most frequently followed) route to recovery may well be a return to that same old model. It is difficult to foresee whether that will happen in the short term, but if the response from the world of tourism goes no further than this, the problem of overcrowding in tourism **destinations**, with people not even having room to breathe on holiday, never mind in their daily lives, **will forcefully remind us of the urgent need to tackle overtourism** and more in general tourism fragilities.

A crucial task thus appears to be finding strategic solutions which can obviate these phenomena which are intrinsic to the structure of tourism today.

In botany, as described in the "Emergence" box, new growth – particularly in times of crisis – can also emerge from a plant's "underlying tissue", a hidden, and often unknown, substrate. To return to our earlier metaphor, this might be said to equate to the sustainable approach, which has also, for far too long, been either hidden or ignored. Understood in these terms, an emergency can open up new possibilities, both with regard to ways of doing business and lifestyle choices. This is not a positing of an alternative economic model, but of one that complements that which currently prevails; it entails defining and accepting constraints – limiting access to, and the exploitation of, natural resources, as a way to restore resilience and mitigate the fragility so dramatically exacerbated by an emergency state.

Let us try to imagine under which conditions this recovery might occur. A territory, its population and the **commons** that are its shared patrimony, available for use and managed according to rules set by the community, are all key elements in any sustainable approach.

> **The commons**
>
> The **commons** are to be understood as that which a community shares: an area in collective use such as cultural and natural resources, open to all members of the community. The commons are owned, but by not by any one person.
> The 'commons' was a key concept in the thought of Elinor Ostrom Nobel prize in Economic Science 1994 the first woman to receive this prize. (1933-2012).

These concepts have been widely analysed in the literature, but largely ignored by both public and private decision makers, who have buried them, archived them as if they were now outdated, no match for globalization.

1.4 Globalization and territory

It is this very globalization that has been to a great extent responsible for the aforementioned breaking points and only a strategic approach which recognises the fundamental importance of sustainability and valorises resilience and the search for a different model to manage sustainability can restore the economic, social and environmental equilibrium of a territory.

A territory, of course, corresponds to a defined geographical area, within which public decisional mechanisms are evaluated and validated by the local community, as are the territory's (collective and individual) social behaviours. This mean that an effort is made to ensure that any decisions taken are compatible with the interests of the community's diverse stakeholders, through active participation and turning individual responsibility into a resource that can be shared by all. In this sense, these behaviours can play a part in better limiting and controlling even the spread of a virus and, by extension, provide greater certainty about when it actually ceases to be dangerous.

If there is agreement on this, it seems realistic to expect that the territory and the local community are more likely to be able to guarantee that it is again possible to live in, or visit, the area without any particular risk to the health of either locals or outsiders. The health of a territory and of its (host) community can thus be understood as "commons" managed locally and shared among both residents and visitors. This prospect can open up the possibility of short holidays for domestic tourists who want to relax and be (come) healthy, an ambition which, at a time like the present, again assumes its original significance, over and above new phenomena such as medical tourism, or the quest for wellbeing.

The four concepts of fragility, resilience, emergency (crisis) and sustainability have always been and very clearly still are intrinsic to the tourism system. Emergencies and crises linked to political instability, terrorism, previous epidemics, economic turmoil and the climate emergency erupt fairly regularly, but tourism has been able to turn itself around and return to business faster than other economic sectors.

This resilience has, in some cases, led to the development of a tourist offer more in synch with the territory itself, recovering and valorising environmental features with the aim of better balancing the exploitation of the territory and its preservation. The sustainability of this model is rooted in the complete rethinking of value systems and the processes based upon them in order to highlight not only the experiential component that a journey can reveal, but also the positive and negative effects on the host territory, positioning itself as a strategic support for the growth of a model of territorial development. The resilience of tourism operators, their capacity to change and to adapt their offer in ways that ensure the overall sustainability of a holiday can become both the instrument and the pathway to address the fragility of the system as a whole.

Resilient, sustainable models therefore provide an opportunity to deal with the fragility of the tourism system, but it must be remembered that their efficacy is best realised when recognised within a new framework of tourism policies that supports the emergence of environmental, social, and economic sustainability as the overarching frame of reference.

The assumption that domestic visitors interested in mountain and sea holidays will represent a considerable segment of the demand in tourist seasons in the short to medium term seems very plausible, with the commonest holiday motivations being the quest for health and wellbeing and physical and psychological regeneration, after months of social isolation and the endless routine of days marked out by online study and/or work exigencies, and with both movement and socialising severely restricted.

The emergence of truly sustainable models could potentially be the tourism system's resilient answer to a structural fragility that has heretofore been taken far too lightly.

1.5 On the road to True Business Sustainability

The path that an organisation, and thus also a tourism destination, needs to follow to achieve True Business Sustainability (TBS) is described by, among others, Elkington (1998) and, more recently and more systematically Dyllick and Muff (2015). The first and crucial step is the transformation of the current economic model, and a shift from traditional to sustainable capitalism. As shown in Figure 1, the framework presents four different business models, starting from the current "business as usual model" totally focused on the maximization of profit and share-holder value, with almost all natural and social costs externalised. The other three business models – all of which are sustainable – provide for three **different degrees of sustainability** (BS 1.0, BS 2.0 and BS 3.0) and different ways to minimize negative externalities. The SB1.0 and SB2.0 models adopt **an inside-out perspective** which consists of little more than relying on increased efficiencies within the current model. In contrast, the SB 3.0 model embraces an **outside-in perspective and requires** businesses to accept that they have to assume their share of societal and environmental responsibilities, thereby becoming part of the solution. In fact, in the **SB 3.0 model, or TBS**, the commons actually become an indispensable value creation for both public and private stakeholders. Only when the shift to an outside-in perspective is made, a business can shift towards different degrees of change with regard to sustainability. While in 1.0 only a business's concerns change, in 2.0 the beneficiaries of value creation also do so, and 3.0 adopts a new organisational perspective.

Figure 1 Typology of Business Sustainability: from an inside-out to an outside-out perspective

Business sustainability Typology	Concerns	Values created	Organizational perspective
Business as usual	Economic concerns	**Shareholder** value	Inside-out
Business **Sustainability 1.0**	**Three dimensional** concerns	**Refined Shareholder** value	Inside-out
Business **Sustainability 2.0**	**Three dimensional** concerns	**Triple bottom line**	Inside-out
Business **Sustainability 3.0**	Starting with **sustainability challenges**	**Creating value for the common good**	**Outside-in**

Source: adapted from Muff & Dyllic, 2014

To sum up, Elkington identifies seven prerequisites for a sustainable capitalist system:

1. free and competitive market;
2. a global shift in human and societal values;
3. transparency through global reporting and disclosure;
4. life-cycle technology and manufacturers' mandatory "cradle to grave" responsibility for their products;
5. a diverse range of organisational partnerships based on mutual trust and cooperation;
6. a combination of two apparently opposite time conceptions: the first managing as much speed as possible in order to operate effectively in the global market, the second adopting the long-term perspective essential for sustainability;
7. corporate governance that includes stakeholders.

Starting from these premises the Dyllick and Muff create the concept of TBS to describe a business that is (consciously) designed with a commitment to resolving societal and environmental issues at its primary goal. The authors believe that not only business models but also the underlying economic model, and consumer behaviour, must change before TBS can be achieved.

To realise TBS, therefore, organisations and tourism destinations must identify resilient strategies capable of experimenting and gradually adapting their business models to the need to reduce the negative impacts of an overtourism which is so resource-hungry and insensitive to ecological and societal equilibria. In this regard, moreover, it is very clear that merely implementing technological and digital changes within the tourist offer will not be enough to persuade and enable businesses to make the adaptations necessary to transform themselves into "truly sustainable" entities.

Bibliography

CARRERA, P. M. & BRIDGES, F. P. (2006). Globalization and healthcare: Understanding health care and medical tourism. *Expert Review of Pharmacoeconomics and Outcomes Research*, *6*, 447-454.

DYLLICK T. MUFF K. (2015). Clarifying the Meaning of Sustainable Business: Introducing a Typology From Business-as-Usual to True Business Sustainability. *Organization & Environment*, March 23, 1–19.

ELKINGTON, J. (1998). Accounting For The Triple Bottom Line. *Measuring Business Excellence*, *2*(3), 18-22, https://doi.org/10.1108/eb025539

Essays, UK. (November 2018) *The fragility of tourism*, https://www.ukessays.com/essays/tourism/tourism-is-fragile.php

FELBER C. (2015). *Economy for the Common Good*. European Economic and Social Committee, September 2015, http://www.eesc.europa.eu/?i=portal.en.eco-opinions.34923

FELBER C. (2015). *Change everything: Creating an Economy for the Common Good*, London, Zeds Books

FELBER C. (2018). *Money – The New Rules of the Game*, New York, Springer

MITCHELL M., CURTIS A. & DAVIDSON P. (2008). Evaluating the process of triple bottom line reporting: Increasing the potential for change. *Local Environment*, *13*(2) 67-80, https://doi.org/10.1080/13549830701581937

ZIBANAI Z. (2014). Is the Tourism Industry a Fragile Heavy Weight? Validation through a Literature Review of Tourism System Shocks. *Journal of Tourism Management Research*, Conscientia Beam, *1*(1), 1-13, https://ideas.repec.org/a/pkp/jotmre/2014p1-13.html

Chapter 2 - Digital Ecosystems

Rodolfo Baggio - https://www.iby.it/pers

2.1 Introduction

The world as we know it today was born, in a sense, fifty years ago, in 1969. In that year three events occurred whose profound effects would not be fully evident until a few years later.

On July 20, the first man set foot on the moon, the culmination of an ambitious, extremely expensive and hectic research and development program. The technological products, but especially the ideas behind them, are still relevant today. On August 15, three days of music at Bethel in upstate New York, better known as the Woodstock festival, which, by common agreement, radically changed the way events and music were done and laid the ground for a new cultural season. On October 20 the first connection between computers at the University of California, Los Angeles (UCLA) and the Stanford Research Institute in Palo Alto mark the birth of ARPANET. Years later it would become that fascinating and pervasive world known as the Internet. To these we might also add the announcement of a novice company, start-up we would say today, called Intel, that introduced the first RAM memory chip, and in a few months it would produce the first CPU (Central Processing Unit, the heart of every computer) on a chip of only a few square centimetres: the famous 4004 that definitely paved the way for miniaturization and the computer products we use today.

But it is above all the emergence and subsequent development, of computer-connection technologies that we can take to symbolize a real revolution, although the other technological births are equally crucial for having, by their progress, ensured that this new world could spread.

After a few years in which ARPANET was the preserve of a few research centres and U.S. government institutions, in 1990 the project was terminated and the Net, now known as the Internet, passed into the hands of private service providers. At the same time, another system was born: the World Wide Web, or rather the technologies behind what today allows millions of people around the world to communicate, inform themselves, and work without spatial or temporal limitations (Naughton, 2016; Yamin, 2019). Right towards the end of that decade, the famous 'dot com bubble' causes an acceleration of the spread of the Internet and the Web, which become established realities, in spite of various detractors, such as Clifford Stoll, with his famous article 'The Internet? Bah! Why Cyberspace Isn't and Never Will Be Nirvana' published in Newsweek in 1995 (Stoll, 1995).

This period clearly shows that we are now in the midst of what philosopher Luciano Floridi has called the fourth revolution, proposing the idea that humans have become informational organisms (inforg) that can interact in the same way with both other biological organisms and engineered artifacts (Floridi, 2014). The conceptpt is that extremely high and pervasive technologies are not just changing our activities, of whatever kind, but that by dramatically changing our means of communication, the way we work, our housing, clothing and food, our methods of transportation, and ultimately the quality of life itself; these changes also profoundly alter beliefs, feelings, moral values, philosophies, and perceptions.

A small but significant change to the relationships between the three worlds that according to Popper represent our relationship with reality: that of physical objects (nature), that of subjective experiences (the mind), and that of the products of the human mind (art, science, technologies), that act by interacting, and in these interactions are structurally and functionally modified (Popper, 1979).

From these considerations Floridi also proposes the concept of *onlife*, which has been very popular in recent times. Namely, that a sharp separation between real and digital, human and machine, online and offline are no longer easily definable. As the first point of the Manifesto of Non- Hostile Communication (https://parole-ostili.it/manifesto/) also states, "Virtual is real."

In fact, Floridi is only the latest exponent, in chronological order, of a line of thought that originated with the science fiction of the 1960s (Philip Dick, Isaac Asimov, Kurt Vonnegut, Robert Sheckley and others) which was systematized and formalized by many scholars at the very time when the Internet began to establish itself as a mass phenomenon.

Several prominent authors (Benedikt, 1991; Markham, 1998; Mitra, 2003; Rheingold, 1993; Waters, 1997), albeit with different tones, assert that, in the words of Barry Wel man (2001: 2031),

"Computer networks are inherently social networks, linking people, organizations, and knowledge. They are social institutions that should not be studied in isolation but as integrated into everyday lives. The proliferation of computer networks has facilitated a deemphasis on group solidarities at work and in the community and afforded a turn to networked societies that are loosely bounded and sparsely knit. The Internet increases people's social capital, increasing contact with friends and relatives who live nearby and far away. New tools must be developed to help people navigate and find knowledge in complex, fragmented, networked societies."

From being a simple tool to improve the efficiency of certain tasks by automating their operations, information technologies have evolved to become a complex phenomenon that plays a crucial role in everyone's lives, and that influences the very essence of business processes not only operationally, but also and, most importantly, from a strategic point of view. It can also be argued (Baldwin, 2012) that the design of any enterprise is constrained and enhanced by technology as the latter influences real-time adaptive capabilities within an organization and between an organization and its environment.

As Werthner and Klein (1999: 1) state, *"Information technology does not only enable, but also induces change"* primarily for activities that depend so heavily on information exchanges such as travel and tourism. Broadly speaking, it could be argued that with the World Wide Web, business and commercial functions have been developed to a good level of sophistication, thus making real the idea of a networked organization, able to function without spatial or temporal constraints.

Moreover, digital marketing channels have greatly influenced the operational practices of businesses, their functional structure, and the way they operate in a globalized economic world. In other words, the increasing pervasiveness of digital tools in our daily lives means that individuals and organizations live in a world at the intersection of the real and the virtual; they influence each other continuously, without substantial differences being perceived.

Now, the question is: is this virtual-real mixture an issue only in people's individual lives or is it also a phenomenon found in complex social and economic structures? In this case, what are the consequences and what indications can be drawn for those who, individuals or organizations, have the task of governing and managing these realities? And how all this relates to that complicated, complex, and barely definable world that involves the countless activities classified as *tourism*?

2.2 Tourism: complexities and key components

Tourism is a highly complex phenomenon. It has been studied in recent decades by several scholars and practitioners who have examined countless aspects from many different perspectives. One of the most important findings has been the realization that a good understanding of the phenomenon requires a systemic approach (Baggio et al., 2010a; Farrell & Twining-Ward, 2004; Sessa, 1988), and a fundamental element for such an undertaking is the study of the involved systems, especially those called tourism destinations. A destination is a central element for any possible treatment, since it is the target of any traveler's activity, and an efficient governance of such a system is considered crucial to exploit the full potential of the phenomenon and ensure a balanced social and economic evolution (Framke, 2002; Fyall & Garrod, 2019; Haugland et al., 2011; Ruhanen et al., 2010).

Moreover, it should be considered that the interaction between the different components of the system – companies, organizations, associations, individuals – is a determining factor for the success not only of the whole destination, but also of individual actors. And this success strongly depends on the efficiency of coordination and integration between the resources, products, and services of the individual entities (Beritelli et al., 2007; Pulido-Fernández & Pulido-Fernández, 2019; Rodríguez-Díaz & Espino-Rodríguez, 2008). Moreover, good destination governance relies on several factors of different nature, where the technological one assumes a relevant importance (Buhalis, 2000; Gretzel et al., 2006; Li et al., 2017).

The complexity of a system is essentially due to the presence of a number of elements (not necessarily the same or similar) connected by dynamic and nonlinear relationships, that is, for which the relationship between actions and results cannot be expressed by a relationship of simple proportionality but calls for more complicated forms. In addition, the system may have hierarchical structures and components endowed with autonomous behaviours that produce configurations, effects and dynamics that are not easily (or at all) predictable or deducible from those of the individual parts and that may span over several temporal and spatial dimensions (Vattam et al., 2011). Moreover, a typical complex system has continuous exchanges with, and is influenced by, the external environment (Baggio, 2008; Johnson, 2009). Frequently cited examples are the brain, the immune system, the climate, metabolic networks, financial markets, the Internet, the World Wide Web, or social structures (Mitchell, 2009).

Complexity science studies these systems starting from the consideration that they should be examined holistically, given the impossibility of understanding all their manifestations as simple compositions of the individual characteristics of its components, as opposed to a traditional reductionist approach that instead adopts the idea that one can divide a system into "simpler" components to be studied separately, and then reconstruct the overall behaviour by recombining the results (Anderson, 1972).

In dealing with the analysis of a complex system, one element seems to play a crucial role: the relationship between dynamic behaviour, functions, and the structural features of the system. This relationship is well known and well-studied in numerous fields. It has contributed to a better understanding of the properties of organic molecules (Le Couteur & Burreson, 2003), metabolic systems (Ma & Zeng, 2003), proteins (Lee et al, 2007), food chains (Pimm, 1982), the human brain (Batista-García-Ramó & Fernández-Verdecia, 2018), the animal and plant kingdoms (Thompson, 1917), or engineered systems such as transportation (Guimerà et al., 2005) or technological architectures (Gubbi et al., 2013). For a complex system, the structural organization (topology) severely affects the range of behaviours available to the system and the dynamics of the processes affecting it.

From what has been said so far, it is not difficult to identify tourism as a complex phenomenon for the understanding of which the study of the systems that are part of it, and mainly of destinations, becomes crucial. Traditionally this is done by looking at their internal components (tourists, residents, businesses, groups, associations, institutions, etc.: the stakeholders), and their relationships (internal or external to the destination) using a reductionist approach. In recent times, however, the complex characteristics of these multifaceted domains – in which the often intricate connections have dynamic and nonlinear characteristics – have been fully recognized, and systemic analysis has begun to produce interesting results from both theoretical and 'practical' perspectives (Baggio, 2008, 2019; Baggio & Sainaghi, 2011; Farrell & Twining-Ward, 2004).

In fact, looking at a tourism destination more closely, one realizes that it is a typical dynamic complex system. Its structure includes a number (usually not small) of elements that develop in response to external and internal stimuli; the relationships connecting these elements are very diverse and range from simple information exchanges to economic and operational relationships, to strategic alliances, all more or less characterized by dynamic nonlinearities, well known and described many times in the literature (Farrell & Twining-Ward, 2004; Faulkner & Russell, 1997; McKercher, 1999). Resistance to external shocks, spontaneous formation of intermediate structures (self-organization), unpredictability of the effects of even minor events, behaviours not reducible in a simple way to those of its components are features that clearly reinforce this interpretation (Baggio, 2008; Sainaghi & Baggio, 2017). One of the visible consequences of this complex nature lies in the major limitations found in all activities of analysing and forecasting trends in tourism phenomena, which, despite the large number of sophisticated methods developed, still show little reliability (Doran, 1999; Smeral, 2007), which is well explainable if one considers 'complexity' as an intrinsic characteristic of the destination system.

This complexity, then, requires a non-superficial rethinking of the approaches and methods of managing or governing a destination. Self-organization, perhaps the most conspicuous feature of a complex system, implies also that its behaviour cannot be completely governed, but that control is, in some way, diffused among many interacting elements (Baggio et al., 2010a; Folke et al., 2005; Liu & Barabási, 2016; Pulido-Fernández & Pulido-Fernández, 2019).

2.3 Tourism destination as a digital ecosystem

If we add to structural considerations the evolutionary characteristics of a destination, characterized by the alternation of phases of growth and stability or even stagnation, we can well adopt the idea that we are facing a real **ecosystem** (Baggio & Del Chiappa, 2014; McKercher, 2005). An ecosystem is essentially determined by the co-evolution between the different existing species and the "food chains" that associate them (Montoya et al, 2003; Polis & Strong, 1996), in our case the exchange relationships (informational, economic, financial, etc.) between the different entities belonging to the different 'species' (businesses) that populate the destination (Rong & Shi, 2014).

These 'physical' elements of the destination are now joined and complemented by infrastructure and technological applications that tend to create a digital environment that on the one hand supports cooperation, knowledge sharing, and open innovation, and on the other hand offers visitors effective and efficient tools to plan their visit and appreciate product and service offerings (Alford & Clarke, 2009; Buhalis, 2003; Xiang, 2018; Zott et al., 2010).

A digital tourism ecosystem is therefore an interconnected system that includes buyers, suppliers and producers of certain products or services, the socioeconomic environment, including the institutional and regulatory framework, and end users (the business ecosystem defined by (Moore, 1996)) combined with the digital world. The latter forms a transparent virtual environment in which open relationships are established between entities and where each entity is involved (Boley & Chang, 2007; Stanley & Briscoe, 2010). Using the network metaphor, in this complex system (Nachira et al., 2007: 8): "the network can be physical and logistical or virtual, can be local or global, or a combination of all the above." The control structure is dynamic and can be formed, modified, and disrupted in response to stimuli from the external environment. In addition, a digital ecosystem oscillates between multiple stable states without having a single optimal or equilibrium configuration (Salmi, 2001).

In a digital ecosystem, therefore, it is possible to recognize two main components: a physical (real) one consisting of the stakeholders of a given economic or industrial sector along with its virtual complement formed by the technological equivalents of these stakeholders. The two components are structurally strongly coupled and co-evolve forming a single system. The real part generates the virtual one, but given the strong relationship between the two, all modifications, changes or perturbations originating in one of them quickly propagate to the whole system (Del Chiappa & Baggio, 2015). Interactions within the combined network can be harmonized through information technologies or other more traditional forms of coordination mechanisms (in-presence or technology-mediated), thus confirming the idea that the offline and online worlds should be considered together (Dini et al., 2008).

Digital ecosystems are of great relevance especially in the case of highly fragmented sectors in which a large number of small and medium-sized companies operate, as in the case of tourism. Indeed, in these circumstances, they are believed to promote content sharing and interactions between companies (Business-to-Business) thus helping the formation of dynamic, efficient, and self-organizing aggregates (Dini et al., 2008), which can produce opportunities for alliance formation and growth for all (Moore, 1993, 1996) and, finally, expand innovative features outside the boundaries of a single company, thereby improving overall competitiveness (Karakas, 2009).

In fact, based on existing research, in a tourism destination – a set of stakeholders (both public and private) embedded in a socioeconomic network (Baggio et al., 2010b) – the performance of a single firm also depends on the behaviour of the others and vice versa (Del Chiappa & Presenza, 2013; Freeman, 1984). Moreover, the performance of a tourism destination as a whole is largely determined by the network of linkages between the various actors and not only by the destination's intrinsic characteristics (March & Wilkinson, 2009; Sainaghi & Baggio, 2014).

Aside from the generic concept used in the popular press to describe the strong relationship between tourism and technologies, the ecosystem perspective is an interesting topic to investigate for understanding the structure and behaviour of a tourism system and of a tourism destination in particular.

2.4 Elementary network theory

The analysis of a complex ecosystem can rely on the work done in a large number of different areas, which has produced a variety of techniques and tools derived from nonlinear time series analysis (Olmedo & Mateos, 2015; Po & Huang, 2008), statistical physics (Cole, 2009) (Provenzano, 2014; Ulubaşoğlu & Hazari, 2004), or agent-based modeling (Amelung et al., 2016; Johnson & Sieber, 2011; Pizzitutti et al., 2014). The most widely used methods, and those that have probably produced the most interesting results in the structural analysis of a destination, belong to the area of **network science**.

Underlying every complex system is a web of interactions that produces effects that are nontrivial, and not understandable by analysing them individually. In other words, there is a network that defines these interactions. Consequently, it is not possible to fully understand a complex system unless this network, which constitutes the true geometry of the system, is described and understood. Theoretical and empirical works done in this field in recent years have shown that, beyond the many differences, the underlying networks of very many systems are governed by common laws that determine and confine their behaviour (Barabási, 2007, 2012; Solé et al., 2003).

The language used to construct a network model of the system originated in the field of the mathematical graph theory (Bollobás, 1998; Diestel, 2016). It is a rigorous language in which the system is formally described in terms of interacting entities (agents), where each of them becomes a node in the network and the different interactions are links (values or not, directional or not, single or multiple, etc.). Moreover, by representing the network as a square matrix (adjacency matrix), whose elements specify whether a pair of nodes is connected or not, we have at our disposal the powerful methods of linear algebra for quantifying many of its features.

This common language, which describes countless complex systems, generates a whole arsenal of tools and concepts typically used in physics to describe collective phenomena. In addition, the methods used, and the interpretation of their results draw on experience from a wide range of fields, making network science an excellent example of how a multidisciplinary effort can provide interesting and valuable results (Barabási, 2016; from Fontoura Costa et al., 2011).

Network science has, in essence, the goal of counting and describing the connections between the elements of any system, whether natural, artificial, social, or economic. Questions asked when adopting this approach involve both empirical and theoretical issues, aiming to understand a network not only as a topological abstraction, but also as a conceptual framework for interpreting a distributed dynamical system (Borgatti et al., 2009; Easley & Kleinberg, 2010).

Models and methods of network science and their framing in the broader class of chaos and complexity theories, as well as statistical mechanics, have given the possibility of describing a very large set of natural, artificial, social and economic phenomena and systems. The topology of a complex network, i.e., the shape and distribution of its elements (nodes and links), is now considered no longer an academic curiosity, but a characteristic and measurable property that has produced a better understanding not only of the mechanisms of formation and evolution of a complex system, but also of numerous dynamic processes such as the spread of viruses or information, the formation and synchronization of opinions. All of these phenomena are strictly dependent on some structural features of a network or of its components (Barabási, 2016).

From this perspective, and especially in a domain such as tourism, this approach is a crucial support for any strategic and operational design activities because they must necessarily be rooted in a deep understanding of a system characteristics. A central issue in design methodologies is the concept of process, which concerns the dynamic changes in information or materials, and the structure of a system has long been known to be deeply connected with the manifestation of some underlying processes (Capra, 1985; Gault et al., 1987; Miller, 1984). Moreover, in the complex global business environment, a good fit between product and service design, the implementation capabilities (the processes) and the organizational structure seems to provide good competitive advantages (Fujimoto, 2007; Jones, 2014; Ottino, 2004).

In tourism and hospitality sectors, network analysis methods have been applied to a diverse range of issues, from the study of topological and dynamic characteristics of destinations, to the study of information and knowledge dissemination mechanisms, to the identification of emerging research issues in the literature, to the behaviour of management teams, to patterns that characterize visitor flows (Baggio, 2017; Casanueva et al., 2016; van der Zee & Vanneste, 2015).

The main analytical methods used for the analysis of a network come, as mentioned, from the mathematical procedures of graph theory, and have seen several improvements and variations, mainly with regard to examining the dynamic characteristics of a network, whether internal or due to external processes.

Numerous metrics have been proposed to describe a network by providing rigorous quantitative assessments that also allow to define dynamic models for the evolution of the system (from Fontoura Costa et al., 2007); the most widely used models for topology characterization are:

- *degree distribution P(k)*: the distribution of the number (and sometimes the type) of links between nodes;

- *average geodesic distance (average path length) L*: the arithmetic mean of the distances (the minimum path joining any two nodes) between nodes in the network;

- *diameter D*: the longest minimum path between two nodes;

- *clustering coefficient C*: represents how well-connected the neighbors of each node are; it gives a measure of the inhomogeneity of the distribution of arcs in a network;

- *efficiency* (locally E*loc* or globally E*glob*): interpretable as a measure of the ability of system elements to exchange information (Latora & Marchiori, 2001);

- *modularity*: the presence of more densely connected regions that actually represent communities within the network. The measure represents the difference in density between connections within a community and those to other nodes in the network (Fortunato & Hric, 2016);

- *assortative mixing coefficient*: which measures the correlation between the degrees of neighboring nodes. If a network is assortative, well- connected elements (with high degree) tend to connect with each other. This quantity, like the clustering coefficient, directly influences the formation of well-connected subnetworks (communities) and offers an indication of their cohesion (Newman, 2002; Quayle et al., 2006).

Based on these metrics, and especially considering the distribution of $P(k)$ degrees, it is possible to classify networks into three broad categories (Amaral et al., 2000):

- *single-scale networks*, in which $P(k)$ has an exponential trend (has the form of a Poisson or Gauss distribution). This class contains the "random" (random: ER) networks described by Erdös and Rényi (1959) and the "small world" (small world: SW) networks proposed by Watts and Strogatz (1998) which are notable for having high aggregation coefficients and low average distances;

- *scale-invariant (scale-free: SF)* networks in which P(k) follows a power law: $P(k) \sim k^{-\gamma}$. The distribution is strongly asymmetric and does not possess an average degree, a scale, that can characterize it (hence the name), some (few) nodes act as hyperconnected "hubs," while the vast majority have few connections. This topology has been found in numerous artificial or natural networks (Barabási & Albert, 1999);

- *large-scale networks*, in which the distribution of connections has a mixed pattern, often a power-law regime is followed by some sudden change (cut-off) with exponential tail decay above a certain value k_C : $P(k) \sim k^{-\gamma} \exp(-k/k_C)$.

Perhaps the most important factor, the one that is most often used to characterize the topology of a network, is the degree distribution of its nodes (see Figure 1). This is usually expressed as a statistical probability distribution P(k): for each degree present in the network, the fraction of nodes possessing that degree (number of links) is calculated.

The power law form is prevalent in the systems studied so far, especially social and economic systems such as a tourism ecosystem. It tells us that the network is the abstract model of a complex system; that is, that we expect to find good self-organizing capabilities, relatively good robustness to perturbations that may affect the system, but also substantial fragility when major hubs (nodes with the largest degrees) are affected. In addition, the "complexity" status means that the window of predictability for system behaviour is relatively small. Therefore, the design of effective governance or systems strategies needs to adopt a dynamic and flexible governance approach rather than a managerial decision-making attitude, which would inevitably clash with the above mentioned characteristics (Baggio et al., 2010a). In this regard, the preparation of a set of simulation tools could provide more reliable information for the preparation of scenarios that form a strong basis for this type of activity (Baggio & Baggio, 2020).

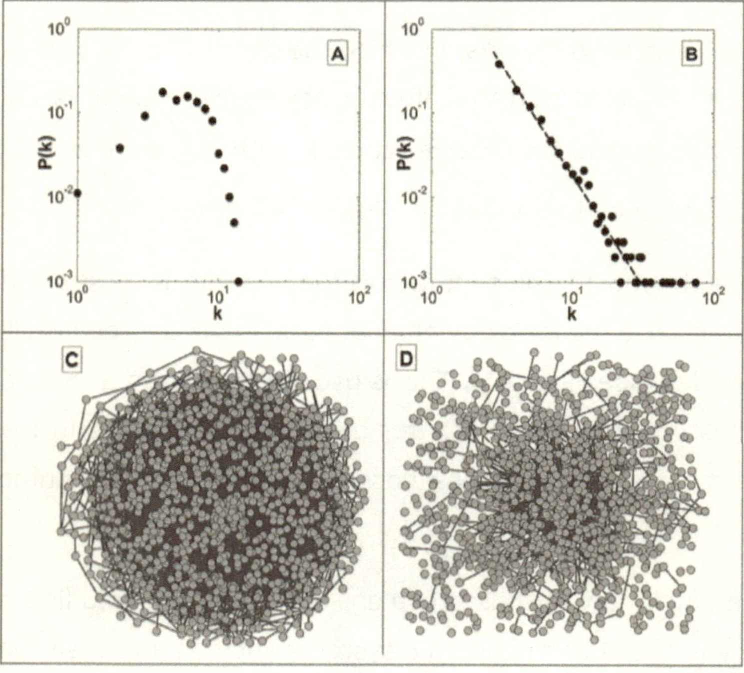

Figure 1 Degree distributions: Poissonian (A) and power-law (B). The distributions are drawn with logarithmic axes to better highlight their shapes. The Poisson distribution shows a characteristic curvature, while the other can be approximated by a straight line (dashed line). The images of the corresponding networks are in C and D, respectively.

The degree distribution also allows us to infer possible mechanisms for a system formation and growth. In particular, among the many mechanisms proposed for scale-invariant networks such as digital ecosystems, two seem particularly suitable. The first is with a preferential mechanism of connection formation (Barabási & Albert, 1999). Also popularly known by the English expression "rich-get-richer", the mechanism involves new connections in a network being formed by an entity with a probability proportional to the degree of the receiving node. In other words, new elements joining the network or newly formed connections are made with higher probability to nodes that already have high degrees. In addition to this basic pattern, similar topologies can be found in networks that do not necessarily grow in terms of nodes or connections but rearrange their connections using preferential attachment criteria (Lee, 2015; Lindquist et al., 2009). This is probably a more realistic explanation for a tourism destination that generally does not experience highly dynamic variation in the number of its components. A second mechanism that can generate a scale-free topology is the result of an optimization process. This mechanism, originally proposed by Mandelbrot (1953), has recently been adapted to the network environment (Carlson & Doyle, 1999). In particular, an interesting variant takes into account local optimization in which agents (nodes) try to maximize the results of their exchanges with partners by having incomplete local information and without full knowledge of other nodes or the structure of the global network (Berger et al., 2004; Pujol et al., 2004). This mechanism is compatible with the preferential mechanism and does not necessarily imply network growth but may result from a series of reconfigurations of connections. A combination of these two mechanisms seems to make good sense when considering the process formation and evolution of relationships in a socioeconomic system such as a tourism destination.

An in-depth study analyses a system on three levels:

- *Local (microscopic)*: the measurement of the properties of individual components (nodes) as described above. Normalized versions of these metrics are usually called centrality.

- *Intermediate (mesoscopic)*: the analysis of possible substructures as modules (or communities); groups of nodes more densely connected to each other than to other parts, or the presence of hierarchies in the topology. The level of separation between different communities is measured by a normalized modularity index Q, varying between 0 (no identifiable communities) to 1 (communities are totally separated).

- *Global (macroscopic)*: the exploration of topological features on a large scale. The main measures are statistical distributions of local metrics and, especially, that of degrees (degree distribution). Other measures used at this level are the average path length (average distance between any two nodes), diameter (longest distance between any two nodes), correlations existing between distributions of different metrics, and average values of microscopic metrics over the entire network.

An important and valuable consequence of an approach such as network science is that representing a system as a network, a numerical abstraction, allows simulations to be performed relatively easily. This means that it is possible to "experiment" with different patterns, configurations and settings or different dynamic processes that would otherwise be impossible for theoretical or practical reasons, as in the case of socioeconomic systems such as a tourism destination.

2.5 Dynamic processes

The most interesting dynamic processes in the study of a destination are those of information dissemination and opinion formation.

Spreading information is a process that has been studied in countless ways, the common metaphor being epidemiological models (Hethcote, 2000; House, 2012; Keeling & Eames, 2005). Such models, in their basic version, consider individuals in a group (population) as susceptible (S) to an infection who then come (I) and can recover (R) from the infection when they acquire some form of immunity. Infection may represent the transfer and acceptance of an idea or message. With regard to information, knowledge or opinion, the most suitable models are those that consider S and I individuals. A first (simple) one is called the SI model. It assumes that susceptible individuals, when exposed to information, accept it and become infected and remain in this state until the end of the process. A second, more elaborate, is the SIS model. Here individuals, once they accept what has been transmitted, have a probability of forgetting, which can simulate the case when information becomes uninteresting or obsolete, or when some other event induces a change in a previously accepted opinion. This model has a well-known threshold τ_C. that depends on the (average) ability of individuals to infect others. The infection process dies when infectivity $\tau < \tau C$. All these processes also depend on the number and distribution of existing relationships in the population.

Another proposal for understanding opinion diffusion is to treat consensus as a particular form of synchronization, a phenomenon that has been very well studied in different contexts by means of simple and effective models. The most popular is that of Kuramoto (1984). Here the elements of a system are thought of as a set of oscillators coupled together. Each oscillator has an intrinsic frequency and a characteristic phase that could be seen as representing the individual's opinion. The links between individuals are given a value that constitutes the coupling intensity between the oscillators. Again, it is shown that when the coupling coefficient K is greater than a critical value KC, which depends on the configuration and characteristics of the system, the whole system synchronizes and all elements oscillate with the same phase, i.e.: a general consensus is reached and opinions are aligned (Arenas et al., 2008; Pluchino et al., 2005).

In addition to designing and performing numerical simulations, an indicator of a network's response to these processes comes from spectral theory. This theory analyses the properties of graphs (connectivity, centrality, etc.) using methods of linear algebra and matrix analysis. Spectral theory has proven to be very effective particularly in the study of dynamic processes affecting a network (Van Mieghem, 2010).

As mentioned, a network can be represented with a square matrix whose elements indicate the existence or non-existence of a connection between two nodes and can have a value (weight) that quantifies some characteristic of the connection (cost, time, distance, etc.). In a square matrix, characteristic quantities called eigenvalues and eigenvectors can be evaluated. Each eigenvalue (as many as there are nodes) corresponds to a vector (eigenvector) whose size is equal to that of the network (as many elements as there are nodes). The ordered set of eigenvalues is called the spectrum of the matrix, and thus of the network. In addition, if the matrix is symmetric, that is, the relations of the network are bidirectional), all the eigenvalues are real numbers.

Eigenvalues and eigenvectors of a graph are closely related to its structural characteristics and summarize its topology (Restrepo et al., 2006). More precisely, eigenvalues contain global information about the network, while eigenvectors contain local information (referring to individual nodes). This is the case, for example, with measures such as Google's PageRank (Brin & Page, 1998), all of which are calculated from the principal eigenvector (the one corresponding to the largest eigenvalue) of the adjacency matrix. Spectral analysis of a network's adjacency matrix can be a useful and, in many cases, a more computationally efficient method for deriving its principal parameters. Among the many interesting results from the large body of studies on spectral graph theory, we use one important result here.

The spectral radius, the largest eigenvalue of the adjacency matrix λ_N plays a crucial role in controlling the dynamic processes described above: diffusion and synchronization. In fact, it has been found that the critical threshold for an epidemic diffusion SIS τ_C for an undirected graph is $\tau_C = 1/\lambda_N$ (Chakrabarti et al., 2008). Regarding synchronization a similar result holds for critical coupling, which turns out to be: $K_C \propto 1/\lambda_N$ (Restrepo et al., 2005).

Regardless of how we model the spread of opinion and the emergence of consensus, the principal eigenvalue of the adjacency matrix shows the properties of these processes on a complex network: the higher its value the lower the critical thresholds, or even: the higher its value, the easier it is to inform and convince the actors in a complex social network.

2.6 Three digital ecosystems

To better understand how the two worlds, real and virtual, are integrated let us use three Italian destinations. One is Elba Island, whose main network characteristics have been analysed in depth elsewhere (Baggio et al., 2010b). The second is Livigno, a mountainous area studied by Mulas (Mulas, 2010), and the third is the marine region of Costa Smeralda – Gallura in Sardinia, described by Del Chiappa and Presenza (Del Chiappa & Presenza, 2013). Elba is a renowned marine destination located off the Tuscan coast and receives about 500,000 tourists who spend about 2.5 million nights a year. Livigno is an Alpine resort in northern Italy near the Swiss border. About 200 thousand tourists arrive mainly in the winter season and spend about one million nights in the destination. Gallura is located on the northeastern coast of Sardinia. The La Maddalena archipelago and the Costa Smeralda, one of Italy's most famous tourism destinations belong to this area. Gallura has about

2 million arrivals and 5 million overnight stays. Most tourists in all destinations are domestic (about 70 percent) and seasonality is quite strong for all.

For all destinations, network elements were classified into two main categories: physical elements, representing "real" businesses and organizations, and virtual elements, the Web sites belonging to tourism operators along with the hyperlinks to them. The Table 1 contains the main dimensions (number of nodes and links) of the three ecosystems analysed along with those of their physical and virtual components.

Table 1 Main characteristics of networks

Destination	Type	Nodes	Links
Elba	Real component	713	1636
	Virtual component	443	494
	Ecosystem	1156	2712
Gallura	Real component	2235	6077
	Virtual component	1477	2165
	Ecosystem	3712	9718
Livigno	Real component	468	1388
	Virtual component	283	566
	Ecosystem	751	2740

As a first analysis, the degree distributions of the various components are calculated (Figure 2, from (Baggio & Del Chiappa, 2014)). The structural analysis shows well the general similarity among these. In fact, the shapes are virtually identical. Fact confirmed by the high and significant correlation values (Spearman): Elba = 0.92, Gallura = 0.97, Livigno = 0.96; and in all cases $p < 10^{-5}$).

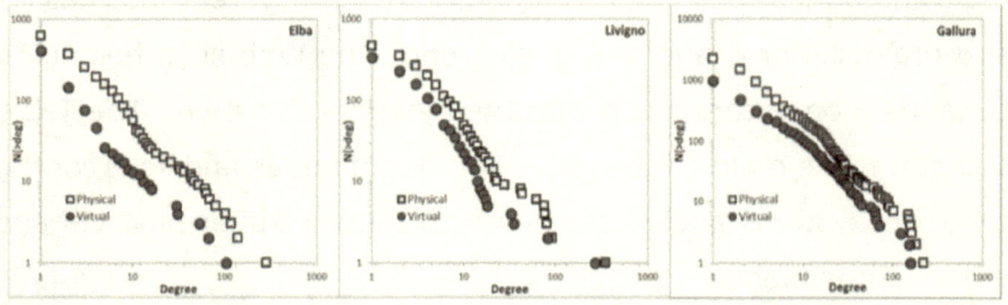

Figure 2 Cumulative degree distribution for the physical and virtual components of the three ecosystems

A second result comes from a mesoscopic examination, through a modularity analysis, to assess the characteristics of internal self-organization. Once the communities in our networks are identified, the proportion of nodes representing the physical and virtual components was measured for each module in order to assess the extent of interrelationship that may be present. The analysis finds a relatively low separation between the communities discovered (Q is generally < 0.5). All modules, however, have a mixed population, and the distribution of both types of elements can be considered fairly uniform (Figure 3, from (Baggio & Del Chiappa, 2014)). The Gini coefficient, which shows the uniformity of distributions between the two types of elements is < 0.2 in all modules (the coefficient is 0 for maximum uniformity, 1 for maximum inequality).

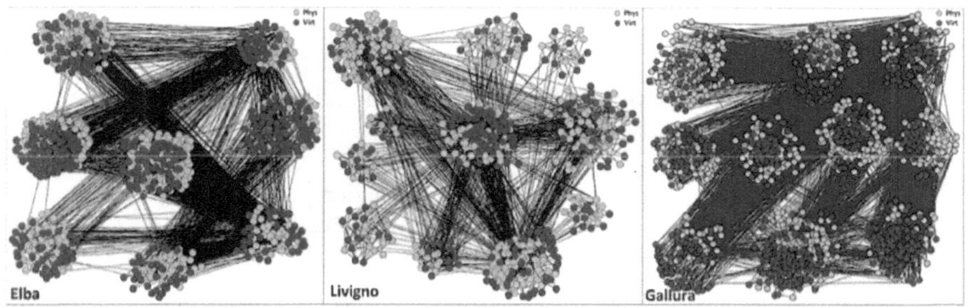

Figure 3 Identified communities.
Different colours indicate physical and virtual components

In addition to static, structural characteristics, we can consider dynamic ones, and we can start with the efficiency of the system with respect to the transmission of information and knowledge or the ability of actors to synchronize their opinions. To do this, measures of local and global efficiency are ideal. Before that, in order to have a more realistic though still very simplified representation, we assign each link a value (weight) representing the cost of connection. Specifically, we give value 1 for a connection between two virtual elements, 2 for a connection between a virtual and a physical element, and 3 for a connection between two physical elements. Although chosen arbitrarily, these values can reasonably represent the actual efforts to establish and maintain these connections, as transaction cost analyses for real and virtual connections and operations have shown (Hagel & Armstrong, 1997; Rayport & Sviokla, 1995; Upton & McAfee, 1996). In other words, we implicitly assume that virtual connections are less expensive than real connections. Indeed, it is well known that the great development in technology has led to a drastic decrease in transaction costs for acquiring and sharing information (Baldwin, 2012).

Table 2 Overall efficiency for weighted networks

Component	Elba	Livigno	Gallura
Real	0.118	0.144	0.113
Ecosystem	0.154	0.188	0.139
Difference	31%	30%	19%

Table 2 shows the values for overall efficiency in the cases examined. It is quite clear how the addition of a virtual component has a positive effect on the entire ecosystem.

If we then consider the possible evolution of dynamic processes, we can proceed with a spectral analysis. As mentioned above, the principal eigenvalue of the adjacency matrix is a reliable summary indicator for assessing network response; the higher its value, the lower the critical thresholds governing the process, the easier it is to inform and convince network actors.

The results for our three networks in Table 3 speak for themselves: the ecosystems, with their combined elements (real and virtual), perform significantly better than the separate components, and better considering the weights assigned to the connections.

Table 3 Principal eigenvalue of the adjacency matrix
of networks and their components

Destination	Weighted ecosystem	Ecosystem	Real component	Virtual component
Elba	34.25	23.26	23.04	11.12
Gallura	59.88	23.09	22.88	19.88
Livigno	51.55	28.25	23.36	12.89

Since the network model lends itself, in a relatively simple way, to be used as a basis for numerical simulation, we can "imagine" what would happen if we changed the existing connections in some way.

The virtual component of a tourism destination is a crucial element for efficient operation of a "smart" destination (Boes et al., 2016). If we accept this idea, it is important to test the contribution of this component and to see whether strengthening it can improve the efficiency of the entire ecosystem.

Given the complexity of the systems, it is impossible to simply add a few new links, so it is necessary to proceed with a simulation in which the connectivity of the virtual component is increased by adding (randomly) a certain proportion of links between virtual elements and between virtual and real elements. In the simulations we consider both the simple (unweighted) and weighted ecosystem and add 5%, 15% and 30% to the base network, respectively. Due to the stochastic nature of the simulations, all results reported here (Table 4) are averaged over ten realizations.

Table 4 Principal eigenvalue of adjacency matrix for various simulations

Destination	Simulation		Weighted ecosystem	Delta	Ecosystem	Delta
Elba	Base		34.25		23.26	
	Base +5% link		34.36	0.34%	23.31	0.23%
	Base	+15% link	34.72	1.39%	23.42	0.70%
	Base	+30% link	35.09	2.46%	23.88	2.71%
Gallura	Base		59.88	--	23.09	--
	Base +5% link		59.88	0.00%	23.15	0.23%
	Base	+15% link	59.98	0.17%	23.26	0.70%
	Base	+30% link	60.24	0.60%	23.68	2.56%
Livigno	Base		51.55	--	28.25	--
	Base +5% link		51.81	0.52%	28.41	0.57%
	Base	+15% link	52.08	1.04%2	28.8	2.02%
	Base	+30% link	52.91	2.65%	29.59	4.73%

These results clearly show the impact of the virtual component on the entire ecosystem. As a reference, for a 30% increase in connectivity, the average improvement is about 2% for the weighted network and 3% for the unweighted case. This can result in an increase in the efficiency of the diffusion process of up to 40% (number of nodes involved or speed of diffusion), depending on the actual network topology (see for example (Chakrabarti et al., 2008). In addition, the results suggest that wider and more intensive use of digital systems can have beneficial effects from a structural point of view, in addition to the other considerations of the favourable effects that digital technologies have on the operation and competitiveness of a tourism destination (Law et al., 2014; Standing et al., 2014).

2.7 Conclusion

Tourism is a highly dynamic and complex phenomenon, involving a multitude of actors of the most diverse types, and a wide variety of activities and processes. In understanding this phenomenon, one of the most important elements is an understanding of its component systems: the destinations. They play a central role in determining the flows and movements of people, and their well-being is considered fundamental for a balanced social and economic growth.

The structure of a destination, like that of any other complex system, is a decisive factor in the performance of the system and determines its functionality and dynamic behaviour. This is important not only for the system itself, but also for all its elements, given the close relationship that exists, especially in the world of tourism, between the performance of the destination and that of the economic and social actors that are part of it.

In this framework, and in the functional structure of a destination, the digital tourism component has a prominent place. The great development, in qualitative and quantitative terms, of information processing technologies has radically changed all the fundamental aspects of the very lives of millions of people in the world. This effect is particularly felt in a domain, such as tourism, which is essentially based on information exchange. In which, that is, the "product" and "service" created and sold do not essentially have a physical dimension but are information that is generated and communicated and flows between the various stakeholders and whose design therefore requires efficient channels for the necessary information exchanges. It goes without saying that the greater the effectiveness and efficiency of these flows, the better the results for a destination and its stakeholders. Hence the idea that a destination can be interpreted as a complex digital ecosystem in which real and virtual aspects complement each other.

Therefore, in considering the relationship between technologies and destinations, between the virtual and physical worlds, one may wonder whether this link, beyond the many investigations that have shown its importance, is only causal or whether there is a deeper reason, in other words, whether there is a "structural" relationship between the two worlds that conditions the functioning of the entire ecosystem.

In this contribution we used the methods of network science, which are considered the most effective for understanding the static, structural, and dynamic characteristics of a complex system.

An examination of three Italian destinations of varying sizes and types has led us to underline the validity of the idea that the technological manifestations of tourism enterprises in a destination play a central role in shaping the characteristics of the entire system. Although limited in number, the analysis conducted with rigorous tools allows us to reliably formulate this conjecture.

The implications of this result are very simple and clear and strongly reaffirm the observation that a clear separation between real and digital, online and offline is now no longer justifiable and that what happens in one of the two worlds is intrinsically and inextricably linked to the other. Moreover, it is, of course, much easier to act on the digital side to change the structure of the system and optimize its configuration so as to better ensure the possibility of achieving goals of efficiency and effectiveness, which are closely linked to the competitiveness and attractiveness of the destination and, ultimately, to the balanced evolution of a tourism ecosystem.

Bibliography

ALFORD, P. & CLARKE, S. (2009). Information technology and tourism: a theoretical critique. *Technovation, 29*, 580-587.

AMELUNG, B., STUDENT, J., NICHOLLS, S., LAMERS, M., BAGGIO, R., BOAVIDA-PORTUGAL, I., JOHNSON, P., DE JONG, E., HOFSTEDE, G.-J., PONS, M., STEIGER, R. & BALBI, S. (2016). The value of agent-based modelling for assessing tourism-environment interactions in the Anthropocene. *Current Opinion in Environmental Sustainability, 23*, 46-53.

ANDERSON, P. W. (1972). More is different. *Science, 177*(4047), 393-396.

ARENAS, A., DÍAZ-GUILERA, A., KURTHS, J., MORENO, Y. & ZHOU, C. (2008). Synchronization in complex networks. *Physics Reports, 469*, 93-153.

BAGGIO, J. A. & BAGGIO, R. (2020). *Modelling and Simulations for Tourism and Hospitality*. Bristol, UK: Channel View.

BAGGIO, R. (2008). Symptoms of complexity in a tourism system. *Tourism Analysis, 13*(1), 1-20.

BAGGIO, R. (2017). Network science and tourism – the state of the art. *Tourism Review, 72*(1), 120-131.

BAGGIO, R. (2019). The science of complexity in the tourism domain: a perspective article. *Tourism Review, 75*(1), 16-19.

BAGGIO, R. & DEL CHIAPPA, G. (2014). Real and virtual relationships in tourism digital ecosystems. *Information Technology and Tourism, 14*(1), 3-19.

BAGGIO, R. & SAINAGHI, R. (2011). Complex and chaotic tourism systems: towards a quantitative approach. *International Journal of Contemporary Hospitality Management, 23*(6), 840-861.

BAGGIO, R., SCOTT, N. & COOPER, C. (2010a). Improving tourism destination governance: a complexity science approach. *Tourism Review, 65*(4), 51-60.

BAGGIO, R., SCOTT, N. & COOPER, C. (2010b). Network science – a review focused on tourism. *Annals of Tourism Research, 37*(3), 802-827.

BALDWIN, C. Y. (2012). Organization design for business ecosystems. *Journal of Organization Design, 1*(1), 20-23.

BARABÁSI, A.-L. (2007). The Architecture of Complexity. *IEEE Control Systems Magazine, 27*(4), 33-42.

BARABÁSI, A.-L. (2012). The network takeover. *Nature Physics, 8*(1), 14-16.

BARABÁSI, A.-L. & ALBERT, R. (1999). Emergence of scaling in random networks. *Science, 286*, 509-512.

BARABÁSI, A. L. (2016). *Network science*. Cambridge, UK, Cambridge University Press.

BATISTA-GARCÍA-RAMÓ, K. & FERNÁNDEZ-VERDECIA, C. I. (2018). What we know about the brain structure–function relationship. *Behavioural Sciences, 8*(4), art. 39.

BENEDIKT, M. (1991). *Cyberspace: First Steps*. Boston, MA, MIT Press.

BERGER, N., BORGS, C., CHAYES, J. T., D'SOUZA, R. M. & KLEINBERG, R. D. (2004). Competition-induced preferential attachment. *Proceedings of the International Colloquium on Automata, Languages, and Programming,* Turku, Finland (12-16 July), 208-221.

BERITELLI, P., BIEGER, T. & LAESSER, C. (2007). Destination governance. Using corporate governance theories as a foundation for effective destination management. *Journal of Travel Research, 46*, 96-107.

BOES, K., BUHALIS, D. & INVERSINI, A. (2016). Smart tourism destinations: ecosystems for tourism destination competitiveness. *International Journal of Tourism Cities, 2*(2), 108-124.

BOLEY, H. & CHANG, E. (2007). Digital Ecosystem: Principles and Semantics. *Proceedings of the 2007 Inaugural IEEE International Conference on Digital Ecosystem and Technologies,* Cairns, Australia. 21-23 February. http://www.tlu.ee/~kpata/uusmeedia/digitalecosystem.pdf

BOLLOBÁS, B. (1998). *Modern Graph Theory*. New York: Springer.

BORGATTI, S. P., MEHRA, A., BRASS, D. J. & LABIANCA, G. (2009). Network Analysis in the Social Sciences. *Science, 323*, 892-895.

BRIN, S. & PAGE, L. (1998). The Anatomy of a Large-Scale Hypertextual (Web) Search Engine. *Computer Networks and ISDN Systems, 30*(1-7), 107-117.

BUHALIS, D. (2000). Marketing the Competitive Destination of the Future. *Tourism Management, 21*, 97-116.

BUHALIS, D. (2003). *eTourism: Information technology for strategic tourism management*. Harlow, UK: Pearson/Prentice-Hall.

CAPRA, F. (1985). Criteria of systems thinking. *Futures*, 475-478.

CARLSON, J. M. & DOYLE, J. C. (1999). Highly optimized tolerance: A mechanism for power laws in designed systems. *Physical Review E, 60*, 1412-1427.

CASANUEVA, C., GALLEGO, Á. & GARCÍA-SÁNCHEZ, M. R. (2016). Social network analysis in tourism. *Current Issues in Tourism, 19*(12), 1190-1209.

CHAKRABARTI, D., WANG, Y., WANG, C., LESKOVEC, J. & FALOUTSOS, C. (2008). Epidemic thresholds in real networks. *ACM Transactions on Information and System Security (TISSEC), 10*(4), art.1.

COLE, S. (2009). A Logistic Tourism Model: Resort Cycles, Globalization, and Chaos. *Annals of Tourism Research, 36*(4), 689-714.

DA FONTOURA COSTA, L., OLIVEIRA, O. N., TRAVIESO, G., RODRIGUES, F. A., VILLAS BOAS, P. R., ANTIQUEIRA, L., VIANA, M. P. & CORREA ROCHA, L. E. (2011). Analysing and modeling real-world phenomena with complex networks: a survey of applications. *Advances in Physics, 60*(3), 329-412.

DA FONTOURA COSTA, L., RODRIGUES, A., TRAVIESO, G. & VILLAS BOAS, P. R. (2007). Characterization of complex networks: A survey of measurements. *Advances in Physics, 56*(1), 167-242.

DEL CHIAPPA, G. & BAGGIO, R. (2015). Knowledge transfer in smart tourism destinations: analysing the effects of a network structure. *Journal of Destination Marketing and Management, 4*(3), 145-150.

DEL CHIAPPA, G. & PRESENZA, A. (2013). The use of Network Analysis to Assess Relationships Among Stakeholders Within a Tourism Destination: An Empirical Investigation on Costa Smeralda-Gallura, Italy. *Tourism Analysis, 18*(1), 1-13.

DIESTEL, R. (2016). *Graph Theory* (5th ed.). New York: Springer. http://diestel-graph-theory.com

DINI, P., LOMBARDO, G., RAZAVI, A. R., MOSCHOYIANNIS, S., KRAUSE, P., NICOLAI, A. & RIVERA LEON, L. (2008). Beyond interoperability to digital ecosystems: regional innovation and socio-economic development led by SMEs. *International Journal of Technological Learning, Innovation and Development, 1*(3), 410-426.

DORAN, C. F. (1999). Why Forecasts Fail: The Limits and Potential of Forecasting in International Relations and Economics. *International Studies Review, 1*(2), 11-41.

EASLEY, D. & KLEINBERG, J. (2010). *Networks, Crowds, and Markets: Reasoning about a Highly Connected World*. Cambridge: Cambridge University Press.

ERDÖS, P. & RÉNYI, A. (1959). On random graphs. *Publicationes Mathematicae (Debrecen), 6*, 290-297.

FARRELL, B. H. & TWINING-WARD, L. (2004). Reconceptualizing Tourism. *Annals of Tourism Research, 31*(2), 274-295.

FAULKNER, B. & RUSSELL, R. (1997). Chaos and complexity in tourism: in search of a new perspective. *Pacific Tourism Review, 1*, 93-102.

FLORIDI, L. (2014). *The fourth revolution: How the infosphere is reshaping human reality*. Oxford, UK: Oxford University Press.

FOLKE, C., HAHN, T., OLSSON, P. & NORBERG, J. (2005). Adaptive governance of social-ecological systems. *Annual Review of Environment and Resources, 30*, 441-473.

FORTUNATO, S. & HRIC, D. (2016). Community detection in networks: A user guide. *Physics reports, 659*, 1-44.

FRAMKE, W. (2002). The Destination as a Concept: A Discussion of the Business-related Perspective versus the Socio-cultural Approach in Tourism Theory. *Scandinavian Journal of Hospitality and Tourism, 2*(2), 92-108.

FREEMAN, R. E. (1984). *Strategic Management: A Stakeholder Approach.* Boston: Pitman.

FUJIMOTO, T. (2007). Architecture-based comparative advantage – a design information view of manufacturing. *Evolutionary and Institutional Economics Review, 4*(1), 55-112.

FYALL, A. & GARROD, B. (2019). Destination management: a perspective article. *Tourism Review,* https://doi.org/10.1108/TR-07-2019-0311

GAULT, F. D., HAMILTON, K. E., HOFFMAN, R. B. & MCINNIS, B. C. (1987). The design approach to socio-economic modelling. *Futures, 19*, 3-25.

GRETZEL, U., FESENMAIER, D. R., FORMICA, S. & O'LEARY, J. T. (2006). Searching for the future: Challenges faced by destination marketing organizations. *Journal of Travel Research, 45*(2), 116-126.

GUBBI, J., BUYYA, R., MARUSIC, S. & PALANISWAMI, M. (2013). Internet of Things (IoT): A vision, architectural elements, and future directions. *Future Generation Computer Systems, 29*(7), 1645-1660.

GUIMERÀ, R., MOSSA, S., TURTSCHI, A. & AMARAL, L. A. N. (2005). The worldwide air transportation network: Anomalous centrality, community structure, and cities' global roles. *Proceedings of the National Academy of Sciences of the United States of America, 102*, 7794-7799.

HAGEL, J. & ARMSTRONG, A. G. (1997). *Net Gain – Expanding markets through virtual communities*. Cambridge, MA: Harvard Business School Press.

HAUGLAND, S. A., NESS, H., GRONSETH, B.-O. & AARSTAD, J. (2011). Development of tourism destinations: An Integrated Multilevel Perspective. *Annals of Tourism Research, 38*(1), 268-290.

HETHCOTE, H. W. (2000). The Mathematics of Infectious Diseases. *SIAM Review, 42*(4), 599-653.

HOUSE, T. (2012). Modelling epidemics on networks. *Contemporary Physics, 53*(3), 213-225.

JOHNSON, N. F. (2009). *Simply complexity: A clear guide to complexity theory*. Oxford, UK: Oneworld Publications.

JOHNSON, P. A. & SIEBER, R. E. (2011). An agent-based approach to providing tourism planning support. *Environment and Planning B: Planning and Design, 38*, 486-504.

JONES, P. H. (2014). Systemic design principles for complex social systems. In G. S. Metcalf (Ed.), *Social systems and design* (pp. 91-128). Tokyo: Springer.

KARAKAS, F. (2009). Welcome to World 2.0: the new digital ecosystem. *Journal of Business Strategy, 30*(4), 23-30.

KEELING, M. J. & EAMES, K. T. D. (2005). Networks and epidemic models. *Journal of the Royal Society Interface, 2*, 295-307.

KURAMOTO, Y. (1984). *Chemical oscillations, waves, and turbulence*. Berlin: Springer-Verlag.

LATORA, V. & MARCHIORI, M. (2001). Efficient behaviour of small-world networks. *Physical Review Letters, 87*(19), 198701.

LAW, R., BUHALIS, D. & COBANOGLU, C. (2014). Progress on information and communication technologies in hospitality and tourism. *International Journal of Contemporary Hospitality Management, 26*(5), 727-750.

LE COUTEUR, P. & BURRESON, J. (2003). *Napoleon's Buttons: 17 Molecules that Changed History*. New York: J.P. Tarcher/Putnam.

LEE, D., REDFERN, O. & ORENGO, C. (2007). Predicting protein function from sequence and structure. *Nature Reviews Molecular Cell Biology, 8*(12), 995-1005.

LEE, S. (2015). Characteristics of a preferentially-attached network grown from a small world. *Journal of the Korean Physical Society, 67*, 1703-1707.

LI, S. C., ROBINSON, P. & ORIADE, A. (2017). Destination marketing: The use of technology since the millennium. *Journal of Destination Marketing & Management, 6*(2), 95-102.

LINDQUIST, J., MA, J., VAN DEN DRIESSCHE, P. & WILLEBOORDSE, F. H. (2009). Network evolution by different rewiring schemes. *Physica D, 238*, 370-378.

LIU, Y. Y. & BARABÁSI, A. L. (2016). Control principles of complex systems. *Reviews of Modern Physics, 88*(3), art. 035006.

MA, H. W. & ZENG, A. P. (2003). The connectivity structure, giant strong component and centrality of metabolic networks. *Bioinformatics, 19*(11), 1423-1430.

MANDELBROT, B. (1953). An informational theory of the statistical structure of languages. In W. Jackson (Ed.), *Communication Theory* (pp. 486-502). Woburn, MA: Butterworth.

MARCH, R. & WILKINSON, I. (2009). Conceptual tools for evaluating tourism partnerships. *Tourism Management, 30*, 455-462.

MARKHAM, A. N. (1998). *Life online: Researching real experience in virtual space*. Lanham, MD: Altamira.

MCKERCHER, B. (1999). A Chaos Approach to Tourism. *Tourism Management, 20*, 425-434.

MCKERCHER, B. (2005). Destinations as Products? A Reflection on Butler's Life cycle. *Tourism Recreation Research, 30*(3), 97-102.

MILLER, T. C. (1984). Towards a conceptual framework for decision-related sciences. *Large Scale Systems, 7*, 197-205.

MITCHELL, M. (2009). *Complexity: A Guided Tour*. Oxford: Oxford University Press.

MITRA, A. (2003). Cybernetic space: Bringing the virtual and real together. *Journal of Interactive Advertising, 3*(2), 1-9.

MONTOYA, J. M., RODRÍGUEZ, M. A. & HAWKINS, B. A. (2003). Food web complexity and higher-level ecosystem services. *Ecology letters, 6*(7), 587-593.

MOORE, J. F. (1993). Predators and prey: the new ecology of competition. *Harvard Business Review, 71*(3), 75-83.

MOORE, J. F. (1996). *The Death of Competition: Leadership and Strategy in the Age of Business Ecosystems*. New York: Harper Business.

MULAS, C. (2010). *Destination Management e Network Analysis: il caso Livigno*. Unpublished MSc Thesis, Libera Università di Lingue e Comunicazione IULM, Milan.

NACHIRA, F., DINI, P., NICOLAI, A., LE LOUARN, M. & RIVERA LÈON, L. (EDS.). (2007). *Digital Business Ecosystems: The Results and the Perspectives of the Digital Business Ecosystem Research and Development Activities in FP6*. Luxembourg: Office for Official Publications of the European Community. http://www.digital-ecosystems.org/dbe-book-2007

NAUGHTON, J. (2016). The evolution of the Internet: from military experiment to General Purpose Technology. *Journal of Cyber Policy, 1*(1), 5-28.

NEWMAN, M. E. J. (2002). Assortative mixing in networks. *Physical Review Letters, 89*(20), 208701.

OLMEDO, E. & MATEOS, R. (2015). Quantitative characterization of chaordic tourist destination. *Tourism Management, 47*, 115-126.

OTTINO, J. M. (2004). Engineering complex systems. *Nature, 427*, 399.

PIMM, S. L. (1982). *Food webs*. Dordrecht: Springer.

PIZZITUTTI, F., MENA, C. F. & WALSH, S. J. (2014). Modelling Tourism in the Galapagos Islands: An Agent-Based Model Approach. *Journal of Artificial Societies and Social Simulation, 17*(1), art.14.

PLUCHINO, A., LATORA, V. & RAPISARDA, A. (2005). Changing Opinions in a Changing World: a New Perspective in Sociophysics. *International Journal of Modern Physics C, 16*(5), 515-531.

PO, W. C. & HUANG, B. N. (2008). Tourism development and economic growth–a nonlinear approach. *Physica A, 387*(22), 5535-5542.

POLIS, G. A. & STRONG, D. R. (1996). Food web complexity and community dynamics. *The American Naturalist, 147*(5), 813-846.

POPPER, K. (1979). *Three worlds. The Tanner Lecture on Human Values (delivered on April 7, 1978)*. Ann Arbor: University of Michigan.

PROVENZANO, D. (2014). Power laws and the market structure of tourism industry. *Empirical Economics, 47*(3), 1055-1066.

PUJOL, J. M., FLACHE, A., SANGÜESA, R. & DELGADO, J. (2004). Emergence of complex networks through local optimization. *Proceedings of the 16th European Conference on Artificial Intelligence, Valencia, Spain (August 22-27)*.

PULIDO-FERNÁNDEZ, M. D. L. C. & PULIDO-FERNÁNDEZ, J. I. (2019). Is There a Good Model for Implementing Governance in Tourist Destinations? The Opinion of Experts. *Sustainability, 11*(12), art. 3342.

QUAYLE, A. P., SIDDIQUI, A. S. & JONES, S. J. M. (2006). Modeling network growth with assortative mixing. *The European Physical Journal B, 50*(4), 617-630.

RAYPORT, J. F. & SVIOKLA, J. J. (1995). Exploiting the Virtual Value Chain. *Harvard Business Review, 73*(6), 75-86.

RESTREPO, J. G., OTT, E. & HUNT, B. R. (2005). Onset of synchronization in large networks of coupled oscillators. *Physical Review E, 71*(3), art.036151.

RESTREPO, J. G., OTT, E. & HUNT, B. R. (2006). Characterizing the dynamical importance of network nodes and links. *Physical Review Letters, 97*, art. 094102.

RHEINGOLD, H. (1993). *The Virtual Community: Homesteading on the Electronic Frontier*. Reading, MA: Addison-Wesley.

RODRÍGUEZ-DÍAZ, M. & ESPINO-RODRÍGUEZ, T. F. (2008). A model of strategic evaluation of a tourism destination based on internal and relational capabilities. *Journal of Travel Research, 46*(4), 368-380.

RONG, K. & SHI, Y. (2014). *Business Ecosystems: Constructs, Configurations, and the Nurturing Process*. London: Palgrave Macmillan.

RUHANEN, L., SCOTT, N., RITCHIE, B. & TKACZYNSKI, A. (2010). Governance: A review and synthesis of the literature. *Tourism Review, 65*(4), 4-16.

SAINAGHI, R. & BAGGIO, R. (2014). Structural social capital and hotel performance: is there a link? *International Journal of Hospitality Management, 37*, 99-110.

SAINAGHI, R. & BAGGIO, R. (2017). Complexity traits and dynamics of tourism destinations. *Tourism Management, 63*, 368-382.

SALMI, O. (2001). Assessing the Industrial Analogy of Ecosystems. In H. Bruun (Ed.), *Technology, society, environment* (pp. 41–52). Helsinki: Helsinki University of Technology Department of Civil and Environmental Engineering.

SESSA, A. (1988). The science of systems for tourism development. *Annals of Tourism Research, 15*(2), 219-235.

SMERAL, E. (2007). World tourism forecasting – keep it quick, simple and dirty. *Tourism Economics, 13*(2), 309-317.

SOLÉ, R. V., FERRER I CANCHO, R., VALVERDE, S. & MONTOYA, J. M. (2003). Selection, Tinkering, and Emergence in Complex Networks. *Complexity, 8*(1), 20-33.

STANDING, C., TANG-TAYE, J.-P. & BOYER, M. (2014). The Impact of the Internet in Travel and Tourism: A Research Review 2001-2010. *Journal of Travel & Tourism Marketing, 31*(1), 82-113.

STANLEY, J. & BRISCOE, G. (2010). The ABC of digital business ecosystems. *Communications Law, 15*(1), 12-25.

STOLL, C. (1995). The Internet? Bah! – Hype alert: Why cyberspace isn't, and will never be, nirvana *Newsweek*. http://www.distributedwork-place.com/DW/News/2010%20News%20January%20-%20June/The%20Internet%20-%20Bah.doc.

THOMPSON, D. W. (1917). *On Growth and Form*. Cambridge: Cambridge University Press.

ULUBAŞOĞLU, M. H. & HAZARI, B. R. (2004). Zipf's law strikes again: the case of tourism. *Journal of Economic Geography, 4*, 459-472.

UPTON, D. & MCAFEE, A. (1996). The Real Virtual Factory. *Harvard Business Review, 74*(4), 123-133.

VAN DER ZEE, E. & VANNESTE, D. (2015). Tourism networks unraveled: a review of the literature on networks in tourism management studies. *Tourism Management Perspectives, 15*, 46-56.

VAN MIEGHEM, P. (2010). *Graph spectra for complex networks*. Cambridge Cambridge University Press.

VATTAM, S. S., GOEL, A. K., RUGABER, S., HMELO-SILVER, C. E., JORDAN, R., GRAY, S. & SINHA, S. (2011). Understanding Complex Natural Systems by Articulating Structure-Behaviour-Function Models. *Educational Technology & Society, 14*(1), 66–81.

WATERS, S. (1997). Ghosting the interface: Cyberspace and spiritualism. *Science as Culture, 6*(3), 414-443.

WATTS, D. J. & STROGATZ, S. H. (1998). Collective dynamics of 'small world' networks. *Nature, 393*(6684), 440-442.

WELLMAN, B. (2001). Computer Networks as Social Networks. *Science 293*, 2031-2034.

WERTHNER, H. & KLEIN, S. (1999). *Information technology and tourism – a challenging relationship*. Wien: Springer.

XIANG, Z. (2018). From digitization to the age of acceleration: On information technology and tourism. *Tourism Management Perspectives, 25*, 147-150.

YAMIN, M. (2019). Information technologies of 21st century and their impact on the society. *International Journal of Information Technology, 11*(4), 759-766.

ZOTT, C., AMIT, R. & MASSA, L. (2010). *The business model: theoretical roots, recent developments, and future research* (working paper, WP-862). Barcelona: University of Navarra-IESE Business School. http://www.iese.edu/research/pdfs/di-0862-e.pdf

Chapter 3 - Sustainability Management

Mariangela Franch - https://webapps.unitn.it/du/it/Persona/PER0004292

3.1 Introduction

The failure thus far to take sustainability issues seriously, and a lack of awareness that the limitless use of a destination's attractions results in the weakening of its competitivity, now means that policy makers and private operators have no choice but to adopt new management strategies.

This involves decisions around new forms of "extended governance" which give local stakeholders a real voice, and, at the operational level, the implementing of specific regulations, such as for example the restriction of access and/or short-term rentals. In other words, the path to address sustainability challenges involves the adoption of a new economic and business model which is environmentally, socially and economically sustainable.

This approach necessarily impacts strategies and policies, both public and private, requiring a medium-term perspective which explicitly distances itself from the "flying visit" tourism model. We must understand that, if a destination is sucked dry, not only will the tourists stop coming, local operators, too, will have no choice but to leave, abandoning the futures which – whether for business or pleasure – could have made the very most of their unique and beautiful home.

3.2 Two contrasting destination management models

A tourist destination must be understood as part of a territory characterized by natural and cultural pull factors and a set of services offered by operators, which seeks to balance the use of the elements that make up these attractions with their ecological and social preservation (Mich & Franch, 2003; Franch, 2004). The destination may comprise a valley, a stretch of coastline or a city, and may sometimes extend across administrative boundaries.

The question of how to manage a destination sustainably has been discussed in the literature since at least the 1990s, and there is general agreement on the existence of two feasible models, as testified by numerous case studies. The **corporate model** largely adopts the managerial thinking of a medium-large sized business and the **community model** that comes from the literature of the industrial district. In practice, there are many hybrid models, which combine the two "pure" management styles in multiple different ways.

The corporate type of management is consistent with the standard model of economic growth which makes no provision for the limiting of resource use and believes that technological advances will enable continued efficient and advantageous economic growth. Business owners and managers are entirely responsible for decision-making and are answerable for the outcomes produced.

In contrast, in the community model, the resources that are managed belong either to individual operators, or public actors and responsibility for their use is shared among the parties involved. Any objective has to factor in both efficiency and the need to preserve the value of the public goods upon which residents' quality of life depends – as, indeed, does the destination's continued appeal to tourists. Thanks too to its multi-stakeholder structure, community type management is more compatible with the sustainable approach to development, based on the three pillars of sustainability: economic, social, and environmental. A destination's managerial processes can only truly be said to be focused on sustainability if the public stakeholder is able to establish limits on the use of the natural resources upon which the destination's tourism development is based, and the operators involved are sufficiently farsighted to accept these limits.

Among the advantages of publicly regulated community multi-stakeholder destination management is that it is well positioned to preserve the territory from the pitfalls of overtourism. In order to manage a destination sustainably it is not, in fact, enough that the management team be sensitive to the issues around sustainability: the actual governance of the destination, too, must be fully sustainable. Moreover, it would be misleading to suggest that technology, especially that linked to the internet and digital platforms, should guide a destination's strategic choices or sustainable management. On the contrary, the current digital oligopoly, and the traditional model of the big corporations upon which it is based – including an adherence to the principle of unlimited growth – can all to easily provide fertile ground for overtourism and other phenomena negative for sustainability.

3.3 Limiting economic growth is not a new idea. Back to the Club of Rome

Half a century ago, in 1972, a book was published which sparked a big debate about humanity's future. It was a report on the overall state of our planet, and it warned us about hypothetical future scenarios. The book, *The Limits to Growth* – which became a best seller, translated into more than thirty languages – was commissioned by the Club of Rome, a group of scientists, humanists and businesspeople united by their shared concern about the situation of the world at the time. Seventeen academics from MIT (the Massachusetts Institute of Technology) were invited by Aurelio Peccei to reflect on what sort of growth would be possible in the future. They came to five conclusions which demonstrated the need to put some limits on global economic growth. In reaching these conclusions, the only function of the environment taken into account was that of provider of raw materials for production and consumption. In presenting his book, Dennis Meadows, the spokesperson for the Club of Rome researchers, particularly underlined that:

> **The Club of Rome** was founded in April 1968 by Aurelio Peccei, the manager of FIAT and the CEO of Olivetti. The group was called the Club of Rome because its first meeting was held in Rome, in the Accademia dei Lincei. The Club's aim was to provide a space in which possible solutions to the problems related to global change could be investigated and worked out.

- There are physical limits to growth which, at the current pace (and this was 1972!), would probably be reached during our children's lifetimes.

- If the short-terms choices we make continue to ignore these limits, they will inevitably be exceeded, with catastrophic consequences.

- The only alternative is to find a balance between population growth and production and what the environment and natural resources can sustain.

- 50-100 years will be needed to reach this balance.

- In pursuing these objectives, each year lost will make an orderly transition to a state of equilibrium more difficult, reducing our options.

The need to limit growth resonated with some businesses, such as Olivetti, in Italy: Peccei, the CEO, introduced some limits, considering them necessary to ensure the company's sustainable development, both in terms of resource use and social impact. This pursuit of a growth model which recognized limits as a factor of intertemporal equilibrium was almost fifty years ahead of its time, anticipating what has now become a common theme. It is a debate which, in recent years, has revealed how crucial it is to take a much broader range of factors into consideration and also to include the natural environment's function as sustainer of life and garbage dump. (Pearce & Turner, 1990); (Pearce, 1994).

Figure 1 The limits of growth 1th. Ed.

If we move from the industrial sector to that of tourism and analyse growth models there, the need to restrict the consumption of natural and social resources can be seen to be inescapable. Indeed, a destination's natural and cultural resources are precisely what attract tourists to it, and the foundations of its uniqueness. To jeopardize the existence of natural attractions by setting no limits on their consumption and without being able to restore them without great difficulty ("it takes a wood", on average, 40-50 years to grow (back), the depletion of soil is irreversible, …) is to follow a logic which will inevitably compromise the entire territory.

> **Commons management**
>
> The term "**common goods**" refers to natural resources and their management which should guarantee their long-term sustainability. Two possibilities are usually considered: public management, to ensure their survival, or privatization, to ensure optimal efficiency of use.
>
> The 2009 Nobel winner Elinor Ostrom has described a third way, which entrusts natural resource management to the communities to which these resources belong. Thus, institutions representing the diverse interests of the local community are responsible for ensuring that the commons are used in ways that are both more consonant with local interests and more efficient in the medium term.

Mass tourism, from this point of view, presents a real threat to the survival of territories and cities, particularly the smaller and/or more historic ones. In the context of our discussion, it is important to remember that natural attractions such as landscapes, aquatic environments, forests and cliffs are almost always public or common goods (Ostrom, 1990) the management of which, given their non-exclusive and non-rivalrous nature, cannot be left to the market. Any decisions made regarding limiting their exploitation for the purposes of tourism must therefore involve public actors, in tandem with the private sector, represented by tourist operators. In other words, a different model of economic development is required, one which we will discuss in the following section. An alternative economic model is needed.

3.4 The standard economic model has to be replaced

As mentioned above, two types of actors – operators and policy makers – are involved in decision making in the tourist sector, and the two do not always share the same objectives.

The businesspeople whose work it is to provide the various services which make up a tourist offer (hospitality, transport, retail, recreational services, etc.), control and manage their productive resources according to a logic of efficiency which dictates that they maximize their short-term profits. Public actors, in contrast, are responsible for managing the territory's natural resources – which define the very nature of the destination's offer. The management of these resources has to follow the precautionary principle: their limited and prudent use is necessary to ensure their medium to long term existence. In the absence of a decision-making space which facilitates dialogue between private and public actors, the predominance of the interests and visions of one or the other can result in outcomes which ignore the wellbeing of the territory and its population, or even threaten their economic survival, as well as the environmental and social survival of the destination itself.

Rigid adherence to a conservationist mindset can mummify a territory, rendering it inaccessible to residents and tourists. The uncontrolled use of natural resources, on the other hand, can lead, in the medium term, to mass consumption, impacting negatively not only on the natural and social environment but also on the economic competitivity of the territory. Overtourism – and all that it entails- is one very real possible consequence of such an approach (Benner, 2019)

One possible way of overcoming the public-private conundrum requires changes to both economic and business models, along the lines of the multi-stakeholder theory proposed by E. Freeman (Freeman, 1984) and informed by the conclusions of E. Ostrom (Ostrom, 1990). Freeman defines the stakeholder as "any group or individual who can affect or is affected by the achievement of the organization's objectives" (pg. 46). Shareholders, suppliers, consumers, local communities, institutions: all are stakeholders.

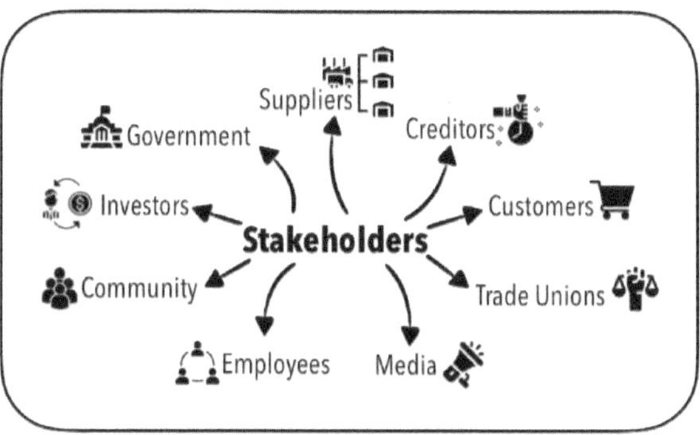

Figure 2 Freeman's stakeholder map – open.edu

Every business creates and destroys value for all of the above actors – and not only for shareholders or the financial backers of the company, unlike in the standard model, where the latter are considered the only stakeholders. Freeman thus widens the frame to include a plurality of actors, all of whom experience the activities of any business with which they have dealings as creating and destroying value. From this perspective, it is not possible to concentrate solely on profit and share value maximization – **total performance** – becomes the business objective, to be pursued in a manner agreed upon by all the different stakeholders. Stakeholder theory thus dramatically

Total performance or **Total Value Created** (TVC) is the result of: CU (Total Value Created for Customers) + SU (Total Value Created for Suppliers) + FI (Total Value Created for Financiers) + EM (Total Value Created for Employees) + CO (Total Value Created for the Community). TVC= f (CU, SU, FI, EM, CO) where "f" is a complex function that combines the value created for each stakeholder into a measure of total value creation.

overturns the rules derived from the application of the standard economic model; furthermore, the theory also, as Freeman suggests, describes a better model for improving the management of any business (Freeman, 2017: 7). From this perspective, the value created by a particular enterprise is no longer solely monetary, it comes to include the social and environmental sustainability fostered in the local community by that business, and also helps to raise general standards of "doing business". Although Freeman's work focuses mainly on industrial firms, his approach is replicable in contexts where a business's economic growth is closely connected to the territory where it operates and is based on the use of public or collective factors of production, as in the case of tourism. In tourism, it is only within the frame of the multi-stakeholder model that the goals of public stakeholders can complement those of private businesses. A multi-stakeholder model based on a public-private management partnership can guarantee that a–territory's resources and medium term competitivity will be preserved, rather than risking their bulimic short-termist consumption.

In this context, public and private stakeholders together are responsible for limiting resource consumption to guarantee that value is not lost and that businesses survive in the medium term. As Freeman might say, the adoption of the multi-stakeholder model is the best strategy for improving the management of a destination and the territory in which it is located.

3.5 A management style consistent with multi-stakeholder theory for the sustainable management of tourism destinations

Until now, we have focused on two prerequisites for sustainable production: management choices have to put limits on resource use and the multi-stakeholder approach has to be recognized as the gold standard in terms of pursuing sustainable long-lasting growth. These assumptions are based on an awareness that both the standard economic model and the idea of unlimited growth must – now more than ever before – face the fact that a business which exceeds certain limits will destroy itself, as happens with overtourism. In order to avoid this, it is necessary to determine a form of governance that will ensure sustainability; such a model can be distinguished from its managerial business and cooperative governance counterparts by the following three characteristics: a) the composition of the governing bodies, b) the organizational model and competences of the management, c) the relationship with digital technologies.

a) In line with stakeholder theory, the governing body should allow space for the representation of all stakeholders involved – both directly and indirectly – in the business's activities, thereby facilitating joint decision-making and the adoption of shared goals. Among these, setting limits to resource use and assuming collective responsibility are crucial for designing and building a sustainable business that incorporates the three dimensions of the *triple bottom line.*[1] The choices will reflect an equilibrium, achieved through negotiation, between the different interests and powers involved.

b) The new governance will result in an organizational model which takes distance from the hierarchical and tends towards the flat and participatory. The necessary competences required of management in this model include the capacity to listen to and value diverse voices, to coordinate and to implement strategic and operational decisions effectively. Human resource management becomes a necessary core competence for management in organizations structured according to this model, which is clearly far more complex than traditional hierarchies.[2]

c) The last, but by no means least important, aspect of the multi-stakeholder model for sustainable management relates to the (inevitable) relationship that all businesses have with technology. Put very briefly, economic theory has always posited technical

---

[1] *"The TBL is an accounting framework that incorporates three dimensions of performance: social, environmental and financial. This differs from traditional reporting frameworks as it includes ecological (or environmental) and social measures that can be difficult to assign appropriate means of measurement".* (Elkington, 1994: 2)

[2] An excellent example of the multistakeholder model and participatory governance is described in the Val di Sole (TN)'s tourist office publication "Summer Val di Sole 2020", which sets out the office's Covid 19 strategy. The strategy was drawn up by a public-private partnership, through a listening process which involved almost 200 local operators. The guidelines and goals of the strategy – born out of an admirably rapid adaptation to the crisis – give tourism operators an opportunity to redefine their offers, taking into account tourists' health and safety needs and the regulations that ensure these are met. https://www.visitvaldisole.it/website_files/generale/Strategia-COVID-estate-2020.pdf

progress as a key driver enabling businesses to overcome limits to growth linked to inadequate or no longer efficient factors of production. Indeed, the prospect of technical progress underpins the very notion of potentially unlimited growth.

Today, technical progress is synonymous with the digital technology that has changed not only how we live but also how we do business. However, digital technology, with its global reach, is no longer just one of a number of crucial growth factors for business: it is now absolutely central to the functioning of a tiny group of businesses who have become sole providers in an essential 21st century service. Rather than simply being another factor of production that supports business innovation, electronic technologies in the digitalized world are now – as never before – moving to centre stage in new business models. The big digital platforms are creating new oligopolies, based on traditional models of unlimited, and unsustainable, growth. Achieving a balance between technology use and sustainability is undoubtedly the most critical issue faced by multi-stakeholder governance models now, as they endeavour to create sustainable businesses. Overcoming this obstacle requires that new (sustainable) digital platforms are incorporated into these models, without distorting the former's structures or goals.

3.6 The sustainable approach to destination management reduces overtourism phenomena

As emphasized in the previous section, the adoption of a sustainable approach to destination management requires that changes be made to the economic- model, and that the management have specific competences, as well as an appropriate business model. The first two elements were discussed in the previous section, here we will focus on the so-called Sustainable Business Model (SBM). Many authors agree that this model must be able to support a management structure in harmony with the three pillars of sustainability (Boons et al, 2013). In particular, Porter and Kramer (Porter & Kramer, 2011) consider that an SBM must include four specific dimensions: value proposition, value creation, value delivery and value capture, which encapsulate the vision of the organization, and the ways in which it creates, delivers and shares value. One absolutely vital question, only touched upon by Porter and Kramer, is how to measure the value created by the application of an SBM. In the standard business model, value is measured in economic terms and is represented by profits and/or share value. In the SBM, alongside economic value, environmental and social value must also be assessed, this requires the ad hoc creation of indicators. Freeman and Ostrom provide useful insights on this matter, since although their approaches differ and they were writing some decades apart, the two authors agree on the dual nature of the goals of sustainable management – shared value creation (the abovementioned TVC) and shared value use/distribution among stakeholders.

A community type tourism destination which adopts the SBM might create, deliver and measure value in ways such as those that will now be outlined: The vision (value proposition) is determined by multi-stakeholder governance: the preservation of the territory's natural and cultural attractions, giving the public stakeholder both the role of negotiator – endeavouring to ensure that the other stakeholders limit their resource use – and that of carrot/stick holder – providing incentives and disincentives for the operators involved in designing and realizing the offer (value creation). Value created can be measured in environmental terms, it might be the preservation of scarce resources, or the enhancing of natural resources (decreasing CO2 levels, improving water quality, etc.). Such value creation can be measured using the environmental life cycle analysis (E-LCA) technique (Filimonau, 2016). Similarly, social value can be assessed by investigating levels of cohesion, the availability of suitable job opportunities in the destination, or the variety and quality of local cultural activities. For private stakeholders, value creation will continue to be measured in terms of economic return. The durability of these returns, achieved through the preservation of the destination's environmental and social value, will be equally important. From another, but related, perspective, value can also be measured by assessing the extent to which negative externalities are reduced by the implementation of sustainable management systems.

And finally, with regard to the sharing of value captured, the SBM model should allow it to be distributed in a manner reflecting the contribution of the various stakeholders to its creation. In some cases, this may be a question of economic distribution (bonuses for employees and partners who have played a part in the realization of this value, more generous contractual terms for suppliers and clients). In other cases, it may involve a (direct or indirect) contribution to the overall sustainability of the destination (investment in green mobility, innovation in management skills for sustainability training, or in programmes promoting responsible and sustainable consumption). In other cases again, it could mean guaranteeing a high quality of life not just for guests but for local residents too.

It seems appropriate to end this chapter with an example of SBM implementation, in a recent post on the Ecobnb.it platform, which testifies to the model's suitability for sustainably managed community type destinations (Nannelli et al, 2020: 8-10):

"Ecobnb is a sustainable tourist marketplace which connects eco-friendly travellers with people offering sustainable accommodation (core value). The value proposition is stated on the platform website and explained by staff during exhibitions, press releases, workshops and conferences. Ecobnb allows individuals to rent their properties (or part of them) using sustainable indicators as prerequisites for access to the platform itself and collaborating with green organizations (value creation). The platform provides green accommodation that may either be self-certified or certified by national and international certification bodies which provide guarantees for the consumer downstream in the value chain (value delivery). The revenue is mediated by the platform which passes payments on to service providers (value capture), while retaining a fee for itself (value capture)".

In conclusion, a sustainable approach to tourism development must become the norm, since it is the only model that can guarantee not only for this generation but above all for future generations, both as tourists and at home, the opportunity to continue to enjoy the natural, historic and cultural beauty that makes each and every destination unique, while also continuing to be able to build businesses which are environmentally and socially, and not just economically, sustainable.

Bibliography

BENNER, M. (2019). *From overtourism to sustainability: A research agenda for qualitative tourism development in the Adriatic*, https://mpra.ub.uni-muenchen.de/92213/

BIEGER, T. (2002). *Management von Destinationen*, München/Wien, Oldenbourg

BOONS, F. & LÜDEKE-FREUND, F. (2013). Business models for sustainable innovation: State-of-the-art and steps towards a research agenda. *Journal of Cleaner Production, 45*, 9-19.

BREUER, H. & LÜDEKE-FREUND, F. (2017). Values-Based Network and Business Model Innovation. *International Journal of Innovation Management, 21*(3), 1-35.

CAPOCCHI, A., VALLONE, C., PIEROTTI, M. & AMADUZZI, A. (2019). Overtourism: A Literature Review to Assess Implications and Future Perspectives. *Sustainability 11*(12), 1-18, https://doi.org/10.3390/su11123303

ELKINGTON, J. (1994). Towards the Sustainable Corporation: Win-Win-Win Business Strategies for Sustainable Development. *California Management Review, 36*(2), 90–100, https://doi.org/10.2307/41165746

FILIMONAU, V. (2016). *Life Cycle Assessment (LCA) and Life Cycle Analysis in Tourism*, Springer, International Publishing, Switzerland.

FRANCH, M., MARTINI, U., BUFFA & F., PARISI, G. (2008). 4L tourism (landscape, leisure, learning and limit): responding to new motivations and expectations of tourists to improve the competitiveness of Alpine destinations in a sustainable way, *Tourism Review, 63*(1), 4-14.

FRANCH, M., MARTINI, U., NOVI INVERARDI, P.L. & BUFFA, F. (2004). The Role of the Regional Tourist Boards in the Destination Marketing Policies: The Case of the Dolomites. *Revista internacional de marketing público y no lucrativo, 1* (2), 113-124, https://doi.org/10.1007/BF02896630

FREEMAN, R. E. (1984). *Strategic management: a stakeholder approach*. Pitman, Boston.

Freeman, R. E. (2009). *Stakeholders: Friedman vs. Freeman Debate*, https://www.youtube.com/watch?v=_sNKIEzYM7M

Getz, D. (1986). Models in tourism planning: Towards integration of theory and practice. *Tourism Management, 7*(1), 21-32.

Lüdeke-Freund, F., Carroux, S., Joyce, A., Massa, L. & Breuer H. (2018). The sustainable business model pattern taxonomy—45 patterns to support sustainability-oriented business model innovation. *Sustainable Production and Consumption, 15*, 145-162, https://doi.org/10.1016/j.spc.2018.06.004

McCool, S. F. & Bosak K. (2019). *A Research Agenda for Sustainable Tourism*. Edward Elgar Publishing, Cheltenham, UK.

Mich, L., Franch, M., & Marzani, P. (2004). Guidelines for excellence in the web sites of tourist destinations: A study of the regional tourist boards in the Alps. *Proceedings e-Society 2004*, 19-26.

Nannelli, M., Della Lucia, M. & Franch, M. (2020). Capturing/Enhancing heritage value by raising sustainability: beyond traditional Business Models in the tourist accommodation service. *Proceeding of Heritage, Tourism and Hospitality International Conference 2020, Mendrisio 6-8 April 2020*, 1-11, http://www.unescochair.usi.ch/hthic2020

Ostrom, E. (1990). *Governing the Commons: The Evolution of Institutions for Collective Action*. Cambridge, Cambridge University Press, UK.

Pearce, D. W. & Turner, R. K. (1990). *Economics of Natural Resources and the Environment*. Johns Hopkins University Press, Baltimora, Maryland.

Pearce, D. W. (1994). The Great Environmental Values Debate. *Environment and Planning A: Economy and Space, 26*(9), 1329–1338, https://doi.org/10.1068/a261329

Pechlaner H., Smeral E. & Matzier K. (2002). Customer value management as a determinant of the competitive position of tourism destinations, *Tourism Review, 57*(4), 15-22, https://doi.org/10.1108/eb058390

Porter, M. E. & Kramer. M. R. (2011). Creating Shared Value. *Harvard Business Review, 89*, Jan-February, 62–77, https://hbr.org/2011/01/the-big-idea-creating-shared-value

Schaltegger, S., Hansen, E. G. & Lüdeke-Freund, F. (2016). Business Models for Sustainability: Origins, Present Research, and Future Avenues. *Organization & Environment, 29*(1), 3–10, https://doi.org/10.1177/1086026615599806

TORRICELLI, M. C. (ED.) (2015). ES-LCA NATURAL HERITAGE: LIFE CYCLE ENVIRONMENTAL AND SOCIAL ANALYSIS OF A PROTECTED AREA (IN ITALIAN) *(VOL. 2)*, FIRENZE, UNIVERSITY PRESS.
WORLD TOURISM ORGANIZATION (2019). *International Tourism Highlights. 2019 Edition*, UNWTO, Madrid, https://doi.org/10.18111/9789284421152

Chapter 4 - Digital Technologies and Systems

Luisa Mich - https://webapps.unitn.it/du/it/Persona/PER0001016

4.1 Introduction

Tourism ecosystems emergencies and crises are most often due to problems related to overtourism. Overtourism appears in many forms, almost all linked to the presence and movements of more tourists than a particular destination can cope with comfortably. The management of tourist flows, through measures that mitigate and change these flows, has thus become a goal common to many of the strategies proposed for dealing with the problems caused by overtourism.

New digital technologies offer us a wide array of tools for collecting and analysing data on tourist movement and behaviours and, more generally, data useful for managing flows in tourism ecosystems. According to the logic of information systems, their use should be planned on the basis of the strategies and measures to be applied, while also taking managerial and organizational aspects into account (Laudon & Laudon, 2020). On the technological level, the Internet and its protocols and services underpin almost all the flow management strategies. The most important is the (World Wide) Web, which made digital systems accessible to everyone, on and in conjunction with all sorts of devices, as now happens with the internet and the web of things.

In this chapter we also propose a method for designing a web strategy for the adoption of measures aimed at preventing, mitigating, or eliminating the effects of overtourism, which Destination Management Organizations (DMOs) and the actors involved in tourist offers can apply, following a 7-step process, with one or more activities, supported by specific models, corresponding to each step.

4.2 Overtourism, strategies and tourist flow management

Overtourism is a multidimensional phenomenon which represents a – current or imminent – challenge for all destinations. The fact that the term is variously defined, and with different emphases, should thus come as no surprise. Almost always, the presence of large numbers of tourists is referred to overtourism – literally "excessive" tourism – and is also translated as "overcrowding", a situation in which limits, in particular those regarding tourist numbers, have been exceeded. As a phenomenon which occurs in time and space, the numbers involved must be contextualized: the same number of tourists may be appropriate in one tourism destination of a certain size but not in another, smaller, destination; equally, if the visitors to a particular attraction are distributed over time their impact is modified. Thus, the most important concept is that of **flow**. The introduction of this concept has enriched tourism research and the vocabulary of

> **Flow**
>
> A term linked to physics and in particular the fluid dynamics, in which it indicates the volume or quantity of liquid which moves across a given area in a given period of time. In the case of overtourism, it refers to tourist movement through a given area.

actors in the sector, going hand in hand with the "static" concept of capacity.

Applied to tourist movements, the concept of flow allows us to understand why many of the strategies proposed for tackling the problems of overtourism are based on the distribution of tourists in time and space and, more generally, on flow management. The first studies of tourist flows – also called tourist "movements" – appeared in the 1990s. More recently, the availability of IT (Information Technologies) for collecting and elaborating data on mobility has led to the use of the terms "traceability", "tracking" and "action-tracking" to express the surveying of movements and activity. These concepts are all useful for explaining how managing flows can help us to implement strategies and measures for dealing with the problems related to overtourism.

Many measures involve interventions linked to the two basic parameters that determine flow: space and time. Others propose actions affecting the tourist offer, yet others consider demand or tourism promotion. Here, we classify the strategies in four groups:

- spatial, based on measures designed to "distribute" *flows across space*;

- temporal, based on measures designed to "distribute" *flows across time*;

- structural, involving *a range of interventions* in the territory and in operators' business models;

- communications, based on *measures to promote*, firstly, the initiatives linked to the spatial, temporal, and structural measures above, but also to foster relations between all the subjects involved: on the demand and offer sides, and with residents.

Examples are given for each of these groups, then the information systems, technologies and data necessary to manage flows are presented[3].

Spatial measures are proposed when specific areas are affected, and it is thus possible to take steps to reduce or even eliminate overcrowding by changing tourist flows[4]. Such measures include:

- *"expanding" the area* in which the tourists move around: promoting or creating attractions, services or events in less crowded areas (in the suburbs of a city, for example);

- distributing visitors along *"alternative routes"* to a destination's attractions and between destinations (for example, by promoting alternative forms of transport, or providing up to date information on waiting and journey times);

- increasing the *"capacity" of tourist attractions and services* (reducing parking spaces and thus incentivizing the use of

---

[3] The examples are taken from an exhaustive classification commissioned by the European Parliament, which consists of seventeen *strategic directions* divided into one hundred and twenty *measures*; the terminology regarding "*measures*" has also been borrowed, https://www.europarl.europa.eu/thinktank/en/document.html?reference=IPOL_STU(2018)629184

[4] The term *nudging* is also used to indicate measures taken to change tourist behaviours and thereby (re)direct flows.

public transport, promoting active transport through the creation of pedestrian or cycle routes, etc);

- decreasing *arrivals and stays in enclosed areas* (discouraging large group visits, cruise ships; putting regulations in place so that rents paid through platforms such as Airbnb are fairly taxed, or introducing an upper limit on the number of visitors or rooms allowed in hotels in the historic centres of cities).

Temporal strategies, based on measures designed to "distribute" flows across time, include:

- encouraging tourists to visit in low season (by cutting prices, putting on events to attract specific visitors, etc);

- giving potential tourists information about *the busiest periods* (suggesting that they change their travel dates to be sure of being able to book entry to the most important sites, for example);

- *reducing the amount of time needed to visit* an attraction (shortening queues or offering virtual visits to museums before the actual visit takes place, etc.);

- changing *opening times* at attractions (by involving associations and/or volunteers in welcoming visitors, for example).

Structural strategies, useful for creating the conditions to manage flows in the mid-long term. These require greater involvement on the part of the public and private stakeholders concerned, and the collation – technically integration – of data on movements with information on preferences and behaviours. They involve measures to:

- incentivize local *business initiatives* that meet sustainable development goals (giving preference to local hoteliers, for instance, or restricting the opening of souvenir shops and supporting local crafts);

- create *tourism development and management plans* in the mid to long term (for example, operators and residents co-creating a strategic plan);

- decrease tourist impact on *natural resources* (introducing taxes on car arrivals, or giving preference to operators with environmental certifications, or introducing fines for polluters, or sharing resource management best practice, etc.);

- focus on *urban planning* measures which take the requirements of both tourists and residents into account (for example, renovating rundown or unsafe areas);

- improve *services and public transport*, increasing "mobility modalities" (for example, by creating bus lanes, or building cycle ways, or designing pedestrian routes).

Communications strategies include measures designed to create an atmosphere in which activities to tackle the problems caused by overtourism, and, more generally, to promote the tourist offer in a way consistent with a vision of sustainable tourism, can be decided, publicized and facilitated. These include:

- encouraging inclusive, innovative *collaborative promotion* (developing advertising campaigns through collaborations with operators and administrators in peripheral areas, or promoting the areas most affected by overtourism less vigorously, for example);

- encouraging *residents* to get involved, even to become "tourists at home" (by giving them reduced rates on public transport and at tourist attractions, for example); good communication with residents is crucial to reduce feelings of tourismphobia (Milano et al, 2019), and for the success of many of the other measures;

- Targeting specific *low-impact tourist segments* and promoting the destination to them, through, if necessary, alternative forms of tourism (focusing on sports that require little infrastructure, for example).

In conclusion, it is important to emphasize that all of the above measures are, to a greater or lesser extent, dependent on the availability of data on tourist flows. Indeed, even the measures that are not explicitly linked to flow management require decisions to be made which rely on information about how tourists move around, and what they do, in a destination. Moreover, the strategies are interlinked: "improving tourist segmentation", for instance, involves measures included in both the spatial and the temporal dispersion group.

4.3 Information systems and digital technologies for tourist flow management

Before introducing the technologies that can be implemented to manage flows, it is necessary to acknowledge that technological or intelligent (smart) solutions are important but cannot solve the congestion problems linked to tourism on their own (UNTWO 2018). Besides, there are difficult decisions to be made and risks to be taken in planning any flow management strategy. First, in fact, one must:

- identify which strategy and what measures are most appropriate, since no solution can be expected to work in all situations;

- remember that the measures have not all been "validated", i.e., successfully applied on the ground, and the data and sources required to evaluate them are not always available.

These factors all point towards the suitability of an **information systems** approach to flow management. In fact, tourist flow management involves the following steps: collecting data on flow characteristics and evolution, integrating this with information about the territory, elaborating the combined data sets, planning interventions on

Information System

According to Laudon&Laudon, "from a business perspective, an Information System is an organizational and managerial solution based on information technology, to a challenge posed by the environment".

the basis of the results of this elaboration in accordance with the chosen measures, deciding on indicators through which to verify the impact of said interventions. For a business, or for any organization, all these activities can be supported by IT, as long as the information system plan takes managerial and organizational factors into account (Laudon & Laudon, 2020). A project for a flow management information system must therefore start by identifying the strategies and measures that have to be adopted (managerial elements) and the "parts to be played", by all the entities, organizations, professionals, businesses etc. who will need to be involved in the process (organizational elements).[5]

The digital technologies and tools available for tackling the problems of overtourism are various, and their analysis allows us to give an initial set of general indications useful for decision makers. Focusing specifically on the data which have to be collected and elaborated, note that these vary in a number of ways:

- The time *period in which data are gathered and elaborated*, which may be "aligned" with the period in which the phenomenon is occurring – in which case we talk about "real time" (for example, the number of people in a room measured by a turnstile which automatically controls the number of entries) – or "deferred time" (for example, seasonal statistics on the tourists in a destination calculated from the data stored in a tourist board's **database**).

> **Database**
>
> An organized collection of data stored and accessed electronically. Databases were introduced as a way of solving the (file system) problems experienced by organizations with their digital archives. DB design uses a range of possible formal techniques; the best known is the relational model, based on data tables. The best-known query language for relational DBs is SQL.

- The "*granularity*" of the data, which ranges from a single datum (or individual) to synthesized data, aggregated or

---

[5] An example of the application of this approach is given in the next section. In some cases, the process has been inverted: new technologies may be analysed to verify whether they are useful for information systems to innovate processes or activities.

estimated; for example, if – using the data from the app on their audio guide – *each* visitor's route through a museum is tracked and this data is used to give the person personalized suggestions during their visit, this is a single datum; if statistical techniques are used to estimate the number of people present in a town square, these are aggregate data (individual data on each person in that location are not needed[6]).

- The *sources* from which they come. Data can come from one or more sources; source is an important factor when deciding what and how many interlocutors should be involved in a plan and what databases, **knowledge bases** or other "sources" (sensors, for example) in place in the territory should be "integrated" (creating a single database, for example) or "interrogated" (creating a web interface that everyone can access in the same way, for example). This is what typically happens with regard to the data necessary for *smart city* projects, in which, for instance, proprietary data from public and private entities are needed in order to optimize access to certain areas, as are the data gathered in real time through detection networks.

> **Knowledge Base**
>
> Knowledge Bases (KB) were introduced to create expert systems. A KB contains facts and rules stored in ways which enable reasoning mechanisms. Later, the term KB was used to indicate the representation of unstructured information in knowledge management systems. The Web is the best-known example.

---

[6] Personal data has to be gathered in accordance with privacy laws, a factor which must always be taken into consideration when designing an information system.

- The *elaboration techniques*, since data analysis can be based on traditional statistical techniques and/or on more innovative ones, using **artificial intelligence**. The latter, which include neural

> **Artificial Intelligence**
>
> According to Marvin Minsky, Artificial Intelligence (AI) is the science of making machines do things which would require intelligence if done by a human.

networks and other computational models used for machine learning are becoming increasingly common, for the analysis of huge volumes of data (big data) looking for patterns of consumer behaviour, or for the analysis of web content (texts or images).

- The *way in which the data is gathered, directly or indirectly*: direct gathering is done by "person counting" systems (turnpikes, for example), tracking tools, sensor networks that use RFID (Radio-Frequency Identification), mobile devices, CCTV systems, drones; indirect gathering, traditionally done through questionnaires or by phone, can now, thanks to the Web, be based on the analysis of content posted online by users, User Generated Content (UGC). The aim is to obtain information about potential tourist segments, tourists' satisfaction, but also their general sentiment (or opinion) about a destination, or one of its tourist attractions. More complex systems based on natural language processing technologies support web reputation monitoring, integrating reviews from different sources, analysing their topics (subjects or issues discussed and opinions expressed) and revealing critical issues that require decision-making.

- The *area in which the data are to be gathered*, crucial for deciding which technologies can be used – these are different depending on whether the area is inside or outside. Tools are available which can be used to manage visitors to a building, for example guests in a hotel, by revealing who is present in which area, integrating the collected data with other information about the visitors.[7] Networks of wireless sensors are generally used in bigger areas, but drones can also be used.

- The *data type*: ranging from numbers to texts, images, video, audio recordings, 3D reconstructions, physical signals (in the case of sensor networks). The Internet and the Web of Things are designed to allow the management of all of these data types; advanced virtual reality (VR) and augmented reality (AR) technologies can be useful for creating virtual visit environments (VR) or to enrich real visits (AR).[8]

More information on how to identify the most useful systems and technologies for flow management can be found by referring to the four groups of measures outlined above (spatial, temporal, structural and communications).

---

[7] See, for example, the system for managing visitors provided by lobbytrack.com.

[8] AR can be used to build knowledge about a locality or attraction, the information is visible in virtual form during the actual visit.

Strategies based on *spatial* measures can use solutions exploiting **Geographical Information Systems**. The latter enable the representation and management of geographical data, visualized on maps – some of which can be extremely data rich – of a particular area. For example, for the measures which require the programming of events in peripheral areas, maps that show any available buildings (such as theatres, sports halls, etc.) and information about how to reach them (journey times on various forms of transport or on foot) are useful in planning. Relevant data both for the planning and the verification of strategies designed to manage flows can be elaborated statistically using GIS. Access to the Web on mobile devices makes maps that include information on a range of things, from tourist attractions to restaurants etc. easily available to the final user. The best-known application, Google Maps, for example, allows one to find the best route to a destination, by various means; destinations can use such applications to suggest alternative routes and/or modes of transport, and much more.[9]

> **Geographical Information System**
>
> GIS enable the gathering, storage, elaboration, visualization, rendering, sharing and presenting of information derived from geographical or georeferenced data.

Using data on mobile device users, traffic flows and hence journey times can be estimated, with information updated in real time. The same data can also be used to provide tourists with a wealth of information: on wait times in queues to enter museums, rush hour periods, the availability of parking spaces, etc. Tips on

---

[9] https:77www.fastcompany/404833528/20-incredible-useful-things-you-didnt-know-google-maps-could-do

how to plan a visit can be further personalized if data on tourists' interests and behaviour is gathered. Tourists' online posts, images, videos – their "content" (UGC), much of which is geo-localized, can be analysed to provide this information.[10]

Traditional data on tourist presences and, above all, on how flows evolve, are necessary to implement effective *temporal* strategies. These data can refer to different times, ranging from real time gathering (using time-metering technologies, for example) to comparisons over longer time spans. For example, to identify the ideal period in which to visit Venice, including a visit to St Mark's Basilica, which has to be booked ahead, or in order to optimize the opening hours of a tourist attraction, a data set on hourly flows over at least one season is required. Systems which register through movement are needed to manage entries into museum rooms: tracking systems and **sensor** networks can be used.[11] To reduce queues, technologies that allow *invisible payments* can be adopted, such as the Italian Telepass system for paying motorway tolls; apps like Uber use stored data to enable ride payments with no direct passenger involvement.[12]

---

[10] PhocusWire ran a *webinar* during which the last topic was called: Combat overtourism with the help of UGC, https://tracommy.com/top-webinars-travel-tourism.

[11] In information systems, this involves supporting planning and verification activities, using MIS (*Management Information Systems*).

[12] An exhaustive review of localization and tracking technologies (including almost 300 bibliographical references) of both commercial and academic relevance is given in (Laoudias et al, 2018).

<table>
<tr><td>

Internet of Things

Margaret Rouse defines the Internet of Things as "a system of interrelated computing devices, mechanical and digital machines, objects, animals or people that are provided with unique identifiers (UIDs) and the ability to transfer data over a network without requiring human-to-human or human-to-computer interaction."

</td></tr>
</table>

Thanks to the **Internet of Things** (IoT) and to the availability of *various types of sensors*, it is possible to create detection networks with as yet largely unexplored potential. In the IoT, objects become primary *producers* of data on real world states and relations, making them available to information systems and web applications with reduced latency and complexity. The IoT makes mass telemetry[13] and the personalized targeting of "things" possible, the three main benefits of which are (Tran, 2019):

1) spatial and temporal trackability of real "objects'

2) collection and analysis of environmental data

3) systems that respond in real time, such as the driverless car.

Detection networks of data on flows that use the IoT, big data analysis, and AI (usually algorithms based on machine learning processes) are also useful when implementing *structural* strategies. These technologies and tools can be used to build systems that support decision-making (*Decision Support System*, DSS), including *Business Intelligence* activities.

---

[13]Telemetry gathers measurements at faraway/inaccessible points and then transmits them automatically to a receptor device for monitoring purposes.

By collecting environmental data (on temperature, for instance), the effects of large numbers of visitors on museum exhibits can be monitored. Wearable devices, such as wearable eye tracking systems, can also be used to monitor what catches people's attention, and for how long (Gregorini et al, 2020).

Types of sensors

As well as position sensors, there are also four other categories (Sharples et al, 2017):

1) movement sensors, which measure acceleration and rota-tion using a 3D reference

2) environmental sensors, which measure environmental conditions such as changes in light levels, temperature, pH, etc.

3) location sensors which measure physical location, such as GPS (Global Positioning System) and nearby objects (used in cars to facilitate parking, for example)

4) body sensors which measure heart rate, fingerprints etc.

Data on heart rate, blood pressure and other physiological parameters collected by wearable devices are also useful for predicting tourist flows, they provide a more detailed picture of individual activities and behaviours than those given by the (external) parameters of time and space (experience sampling methods) (Shoval, 2018). On a wider scale, the IoT can provide urban planners with useful data on the needs of both tourists and residents (Shoval et al., 2018). An innovative project based on the IoT is described in the box below.

The Internet of Things for a Smart green region

In 2019 in South Tyrol, a region in the north of Italy, an innovative project based on the Internet of Things began: the creation of a network of 3,500 beacons (sensors that are not connected to the Internet and have a one-to-one code picked up using Bluetooth on a smartphone). The aim is to build an infra-structure covering the entire territory of the autonomous Province of Bolzano. It is the first entirely public network of its kind in Italy, based on a free, open-access platform: the province hopes it will serve as a model smart green region. The network enables the creation of new services and innovative business models. Since the sensors detect a phone's exact position, even in enclosed environments (unlike GPS), this position reading can be used by official apps to provide the users with location-based services. One of the first applications using these data is the "South Tyrol Mobile Guide" which give tourists useful information, on such aspects as nearby services and attractions, and current weather and traffic conditions. Among the applications for use in enclosed environments, the Bolzano Fair uses the network to guide visitors around the pavilions or towards specific exhibitors. Another app guides visitors around the botanical gardens at Castel Trauttmansdorff in Merano.

Indeed, the very concept of the **smart city** would not be possible without the IoT. Here, the data model used is that of open data, i.e., information – usually gathered by public entities – which is available to everyone (maps are a classic example). The box below provides examples of various smart city projects across Europe.

Smart city

An urban area in which sensors and other devices are used to gather data which, integrated and analysed in conjunction with those held by public administrations, can be used to manage resources and services.

Sensors in cities

In Verona "head-counter" sensors, consisting of a telecamera with a software card, have been installed to measure the flow of passers-by and traffic in the area around Porta Nuova, where restoration work is being done. As well as counting people and vehicles and calculating how much time they spend in the area, these devices – thanks to AI algorithms – can establish the degree of attention paid by passers-by and estimate their age and gender, and then analyse these data without having to send them to a server (thus safeguarding privacy). All the data are used to ascertain the impact on different passer-by profiles of the hoarding (advertising a private company) which surrounds the work site. Sensors like this can be useful in many other applications; the data gathered can facilitate traffic management, transport networks, waste collection, electricity, and water provision. In Holland, as part of the CityPulse project[14] telecameras and microphones have been installed on 15 lamp posts on a street in the centre of Eindhoven. This makes it possible to detect movements and noise levels and thus to help prevent street violence; it also means that the streetlamps only light up when they detect the approach of a pedestrian, thereby conserving energy. In Bari (south of Italy) not only sensors and video cameras but also drones are used to control the movements of cargo ships and people in the port area and to measure their environmental impact.[15] In Barcelona, an open-source platform of sensors and actuators[16,] Sentilo, gathers data on traffic, noise, air quality, water consumption etc. to improve public transport and waste collection services, among other things. Vienna installed traffic lights that optimize wait times in line with pedestrian and driver behaviour.17 Yet another plan envisions the elimination of traffic lights, by making it possible for the vehicles themselves to 'know' when they can proceed. Moreover, in future cities with driverless vehicles, hybrid public-private transport systems could be created, to reduce the periods in which private cars are sitting idle, and thus also the number of parking places required.[18]

Action-tracking systems can also be used to assess the impact of an event on the host territory, allowing administrations to optimize their investments. This has been done in a number of cities. In Trento, a city in the North of Italy, a platform to collect data on the use of the tourist offer and tourists' spending behaviours was designed using RFID technology (Frith, 2019) to calculate the

---

[14] http://www.ict-citypulse.eu

[15] https://www.dbagroup.it/it/dba-ems

[16] https://ajuntament.barcelona.cat

[17]https://www.themayor.eu/en/a/view/traffic-lights-that-think-and-communicate-improve-traffic-flow-in-vienna-2404

[18] https://corriereinnovazione.corriere.it/cards/come-sara-fatta-citta-futuro-ce-spiega-l-architetto-carlo-ratti/auto-garage.shtml

economic impact of two important international festivals, the Festival of Economics[19] and the Mountain Film Festival[20].The box below gives further details.

The RFID for Festivals projects

Both festivals involve significant investment. Data on the return on investments are crucial for organizers. RFID technologies were applied at the Trento Festival of Economics – an international event first held in 2006 – to gather data with which to assess the festival's economic impact. The theoretical model takes three types of impact into account: direct, indirect, and induced. The first level of analysis requires data both on the costs sustained by the organizers and on what people who visited the city for the event spent. The other two types of impact are calculated from the results of the first analysis. The project involved developing an action-tracking system based on the circulation of the Trento Card, an RFID city card which was given to a significant proportion of the festival participants (visitors and speakers); data was collected on the card recipients to build profiles of them. 35 recording points – including museums and other outlets – were chosen to track spending behaviours. The results of the evaluation both validated the platform and the chosen method and showed that the festival had a very positive economic impact on the city.[21] The overall sustainability of the event could also be assessed, using environmental data and data on the perceptions of city residents.

Videogames like SimCity can provide realistic simulations of urban landscapes helpful in decision making.[22] Measures to incentivize sustainable development friendly entrepreneurial initiatives on the part of residents can benefit from e-commerce and e-business technologies, building platforms on which to valorise local

---

[19] https://2021.festivaleconomia.eu/en.html

[20] https://trentofestival.it/en

[21] A detailed description of the RFID project for the 2008 Festival can be found in Della Lucia et al., 2010).

[22] http://www.simcity.com

commerce. One such project is *Venezia Autentica*, which involves Venetian artisans, restauranteurs, and professionals.[23] A booking platform worth noting is Fairbnb: it is managed by a cooperative and, in turn, works with local cooperatives, thus providing an alternative to the Airbnb model.[24]

The final group of strategies for tackling overtourism, the *communicative*, includes measures which require IT support at all sorts of interaction – from communication, to coordination, to collaboration and cooperation – involving tourism stakeholders: tourism operators, of course, but also tourists, residents, local associations (cultural, sporting); transport companies, public administrators etc. Tools for exchanging information, sharing material, collaborating, training, are all needed. The systems and technologies available to this end range from email and apps like VoIP to platforms that encourage cooperation and/or manage knowledge (Wikipedia is the best-known example of the latter). In the area of information systems for marketing, platforms for participatory planning and design are also important. All these systems and applications enable both the gathering and the production of useful data for managing flows. The Web is the shared interface for many of these, which means that it is important for a destination to have a web presence strategy that includes support for tourist flow management in its design.

---

[23] https://veneziaautentica.com
[24] https://fairbnb.coop

4.4 A method for designing a web presence

In designing a destination's web presence, the question that first arises is: "which websites and tools ("spaces", for simplicity's sake) can support this destination's strategies?". When using the Web to deal (also) with the problems caused by overtourism, the *first step* in planning the web presence strategy must be to examine how overtourism manifests in that destination. The *second step* is to identify what measures can be taken to tackle these manifestations and which "subjects" can participate in the application of the agreed measures. The *third step* is to decide which information technologies are most appropriate, based on the first two steps and on how information systems functionalities can be implemented on the destination's web spaces. The *fourth step* is to create a map and a matrix of the web presence to check its coherence with the objectives drawn up in the first step; in these models the web spaces and their links and some data on their "vitality" are represented. It may sometimes be helpful at this stage to create a map of "linking in web sites" to check whether or not the web sites which should contain a link to the destination sites on the map actually do so (for example, the link to the B2C, Business to Consumer web site, for a city's tourism should be present on the site of the region where the city is located, and on any sites involved in the design of tourist products etc.). The *fifth step* is the maintenance of the web presence: ordinary maintenance (to ensure that the web spaces are functioning properly; a range of software can be used) and extra-ordinary maintenance (i.e., changes to increase security levels or to bring terms of service in line with new privacy norms) of the sites and the web tools that make up the web presence strategy. The *sixth step* is the quality evaluation of the web spaces: a range of evaluation methods and approaches can be employed, including those derived from the meta-model 7Loci (whose name we have adopted also for the method proposed here) (Mich, 2017; Mich & Kiyavitskaya, 2011).The *seventh*, and last, step is to schedule the resources necessary for realizing the web presence strategy and the evaluation of its impact in relation to the problems identified and the measures adopted to deal with them. Data on user navigation (analytics, as offered by Google, for instance) are particularly useful in this regard; specific indicators for monitoring the impact of the web strategy can also be determined. At another level, it may be useful to analyse online reputation or sentiment, both in relation to specific elements (a new event, an advertising campaign, etc.) and more generally (how overcrowded the destination is perceived to be, etc.).

The activities in the first three steps correspond to those involved in creating an information system and can be represented in a graph – the Laudon & Laudon model – an example of which is given in the next section about the method's application to the city of Munich in the south of Germany.

The 7 steps of the method summarized in Table 1.

Table 1 The 7Loci method for designing a web presence strategy

Step	Description	Models and tools
Quis	Business challenges, problems	Laudon&Laudon
Quid	Strategies, measures & actors	Laudon&Laudon
Cur	Technologies & IS functionalities	Laudon&Laudon
Ubi	Web spaces	Maps, web presence matrixes, mentions
Quando	Operability, maintenance	Checkers, validators, testers
Quomodo	Web sites quality	7Loci meta-model
Quibus Auxiliis	Impacts and web reputation	Analytics, web reputation monitoring

4.5 The 7Loci method applied: overtourism in Munich

In the remainder of the chapter, we investigate an example of the 7Loci method in action, simulating a project for the city of Munich in January 2020.

Munich has seen a considerable rise in tourist numbers in recent years. In a strategy statement published in 2012, the city's tourist board declared that by 2020 Munich would "be the most attractive European city for those seeking culture, enjoyment, and a zest for life, while also offering visitors a unique opportunity to take part in the life of the city."[25] Best known for its *Oktoberfest*, Munich offers many other attractions and activities and boasts an extensive and efficient public transport system. It has a population of over 1.5 million, about one third of whom are foreigners; including the suburbs, the population rises to 5 million. In 2018, the year in which it was declared the city with the highest life quality in the

---

[25] https://www.munich.travel/en/topics/about-us/tourism-strategy

world, Munich welcomed almost 8.3 million tourists (half of whom came from abroad) for over 17 million overnight stays[26] (2,992,527 and 7,034,040, respectively in 2020)[27].

a. The first step: identifying challenges and problems

According to a recent report, Munich is one of those cities with "balanced dynamics" in which tourism still has space for growth.[28] Nevertheless, official data give a ratio of 2.65 tourists to every inhabitant,[29] and show that the threshold (generally considered to be critical) of 10 overnight stays per inhabitant has been crossed, increasing by more than 100% since 2003. These data push Munich out of the set of "balanced" cities (where the earlier study had positioned it) and into that of cities "under pressure".[30] Moreover, a survey of residents' perceptions of tourism revealed that a significant proportion (almost half of the residents questioned) feel that there are too many tourists and that their presence negatively impacts the city's liveability; another phenomenon flagged as

---

[26] https://www.tuttobaviera.it/statistiche-monaco

[27] https://www.statista.com/statistics/569562/key-figures-tourism-munich-germany/

[28] "Cities are often financial hubs with a lower share of leisure compared to business travel, but they also have an established tourism infrastructure and potential for Travel & Tourism growth." https://www.wttc.org/publications/2019/destination-2030

[29] https://www.official-esta.com/information/reports/cities-with-most-tourists

[30] https://www.rolandberger.com/en/Publications/Overtourism-in-Europe's-cities.html

critical is linked to the "grey market" in rentals, with platforms like Airbnb driving an increase in rents and forcing residents to abandon the city centre; furthermore, residents say that renters are a nuisance and often do not differentiate waste correctly. (Namberger et al, 2019) The aforementioned data and the residents' perceptions of tourism both indicate that Munich risks ending up on the overtourism map sooner rather than later.[31]

b. The second step: strategies, measures and actors

Since the sheer number of tourists has been shown to be the most critical factor, the München Tourismus Buro could implement strategies to limit arrivals during the city's biggest events, such as the Oktoberfest (6.3 million visitors in 2018) and important football games. In the case of the Oktoberfest, Munich could twin itself with other cities that hold similar events, making them "official", as well as assessing the impact of the Oktoberfest Barometer[32]. At the same time, it could join other cities in attempting to regulate online accommodation rental platforms and incentivize other forms of accommodation, by using the city's "Muenchen card", for example. Furthermore, it could launch a tourist awareness campaign, to advise tourists on how to behave so as not to disturb the residents, how to differentiate waste, etc. For all these measures, the appropriate subjects to involve must be identified: in this case, not only

---

[31] https://www.responsibletravel.com/copy/overtourism-map

[32] https://www.oktoberfest.de/en/information/service-for-visitors/the-best-time-to-visit-oktoberfest-the-oktoberfest-barometer

operators and residents but also those entities authorized to decide on forms of control and incentives.

c. The third step: technologies and IS functionalities

A web presence strategy can use a range of technologies and platforms to support whichever measures have been chosen to mitigate the current and future effects of overtourism. As well as communications published on the official website or the social media platforms where *München Tourismus* has its online presence, it might be useful to develop an *app* for specific needs, such as those mentioned in the previous step: rules of behaviour, correct waste differentiation. In general, all the technologies described in this chapter are potentially useful. It is up to decision makers, together with Web engineers, to identify which technologies are likely to be most appropriate for whichever strategies and measures have been chosen.

d. The fourth step: designing a web presence

Munich's current web presence can be modelled on a map (Fig. 1), highlighting the sites – and their links – on which the destination is being promoted. Looking at the map, it is possible to glean helpful clues for improving the city's web presence, based on a consideration of the objectives connected to the previous step. The map can be accompanied by a matrix (Table 2) which gathers information on the various sites: addresses, popularity, and any other information useful for identifying problems and suggesting improvements.

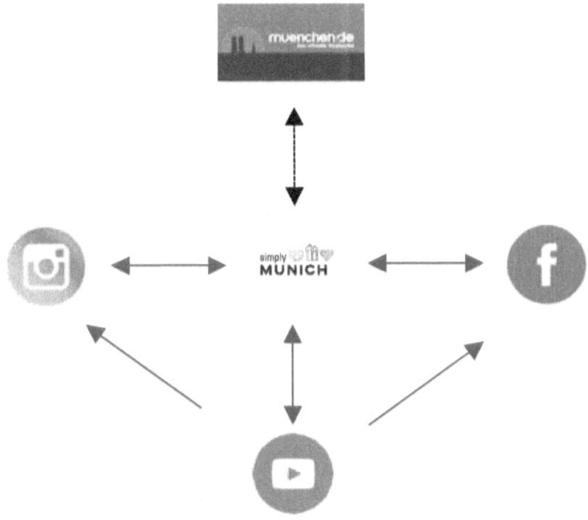

Figure 1 Map of Munich's web presence as a tourism destination
(February 3, 2020)

Table 2 Matrix of Munich's web presence as a tourism destination
(February 3 2020)

	Official tourism website	Facebook	YouTube	Instagram
Addresses	www.muenchen.travel[en][www.simply-munich.com, www.munich.travel] www.muenchen.de	https://www.facebook.com/simplymunich	https://www.youtube.com/channel/UCPYZ-RMmtZ1gbEQ9tnY-hgnVg	https://www.instagram.com/simplymunich
Data on "members", views		10,204 *likes* 10,654 *follows*	11,101 *views* since March 12 2018	11,400 *followers*
Updates		1 day ago	1 week ago	1 day ago
Official website		x	x	x
Facebook	x			
YouTube	x	x		x
Instagram	x			

One issue that emerges from these representations regards the fact that Munich has two sites: one supporting its function as the capital city of Bavaria, the other that of the tourist office. The former, in fact, particularly in its English version, deals primarily with tourism promotion, with all the services and other information that one would expect to find on an administration's website very much in second place. The site dedicated entirely to tourism is called SimplyMunich, EinfachMünchen in German. The tourist office and the municipality should clarify the respective roles of the two sites and, if necessary, redistribute and reformulate the content on the two sites. Both have a profile on the most popular social media sites: Facebook, YouTube, and Instagram. The first also has a Twitter account. For simplicity's sake, only SimplyMunich's profiles are shown on the map and in the matrix. The city's web presence strategy should be given a general overhaul, with new designs that better reflect the different missions of the two organizations concerned. The choice not to link the official channel on YouTube with the Facebook and Instagram profiles makes sense: the objective is not to have a fully connected map, but to interconnect the spaces according to their roles.

Finally, as part of this step it is useful to see if Munich's tourism site is linked by the sites of the tourist entities and organizations which can reasonably be expected to mention it. The same applies to platforms like Wikipedia, Wikitravel and other important online sources for potential tourists. SimplyMunich is linked by the municipal site (www.muenchen.de – the two sites also contain some of the same content); by the provincial site (Land Bayern, www.bavaria.by, although the link does not work), and by the

Germany's national tourism board site (www.germany.travel). Munich also has a Wikitravel entry, and one on Tripadvisor. Muenchen Tourismus should establish whether or not there are other sites upon which it would be opportune to appear, particularly those of entities whom it would be advantageous to involve in implementing the strategies identified in the second step.

e. The fifth step: operability and maintenance

A very elegant metaphor expresses an important characteristic of the Web: it suggests that sites should be designed and maintained as if they were gardens. (Lowe, 1999)

The objective of this step is to check that all the web spaces on which Munich's online presence strategy is based are functioning correctly. An initial check can be carried out using tools that are also available to end users. These include software that checks the links to a site (checkers), or the compatibility of its codes with Web standards (validators).[33] It is also important to check that privacy laws are being followed, if security levels are being ensured etc. If other devices are included, such as some of the sensors described earlier in this chapter, checks and maintenance on all "objects" connected to the Web (IoT) should be factored in.

---

[33] www.w3.org

f. The sixth step: evaluating the quality of the web spaces

The quality of the sites in which Munich is investing for tourism can be assessed by applying quality evaluation schema based on the meta model 7Loci (Mich 2017) in order to highlight where improvements can be made and also to flag up any changes necessary for eventual measures to deal with the problems of overtourism. Examples of problems with and suggestions for the SimplyMunich site are given in Table 3. A similar analysis can be done on the Facebook, Instagram and YouTube profiles, taking into account their particular characteristics, of course. (Mich & Baggio, 2015)

The web site was designed recently using state of the art technologies; the layout is simple and effective (Fig. 2). The logo is in two languages (usually to be avoided, but since half of Munich's tourists are German, justifiable) and the pictograph contains elements which are also used within the site, to signpost the various offers available. It is easy to navigate, and mobile friendly. However, the order in which the different activities, events and services are set out could be reconsidered, particularly through the implementation of personalization strategies. It might be better not to advertise low-cost packages on the homepage, for instance, and instead to highlight the city card by giving it prominence. The apps for organizing a city visit are only available on the municipal site. In general, given that the city's public transport system and services are very efficient, and do not require any structural changes, well-targeted online communications would probably suffice to ensure that many of the measures suggested in the literature were realised.

The overall layout could be rethought, bearing in mind that the objective is not to increase tourist numbers but to improve tourist/resident relationships and to reduce or contain tourist flows linked to specific events. So, for example, videos containing practical tips or instructions could replace those currently on YouTube, which, although very well made and attractive, focus almost entirely on promotion, and have rather few views.

Table 3 Examples of quality issues on the muenchen.travel (simplymunich) site (February 2020)

Dimension	Description	Problems
Quis	Identity	No direct references to sustainability or to initiatives to avoid overtourism
Quid	Content	Promotion of low-cost packages
Cur	Services	No apps for visiting the city and its surroundings
Ubi	Identification	Having two "tourism" sites is confusing
Quando	Maintenance	Christmas markets still being advertised at the beginning of February
Quomodo	Usability	Long texts (e.g. to describe the various city cards)
Quibus Auxiliis	Feasibility	Similar features to those on "competing" sites, such as munich-touristinfo.de (see www.alexa.com/siteinfo/munich.travel)

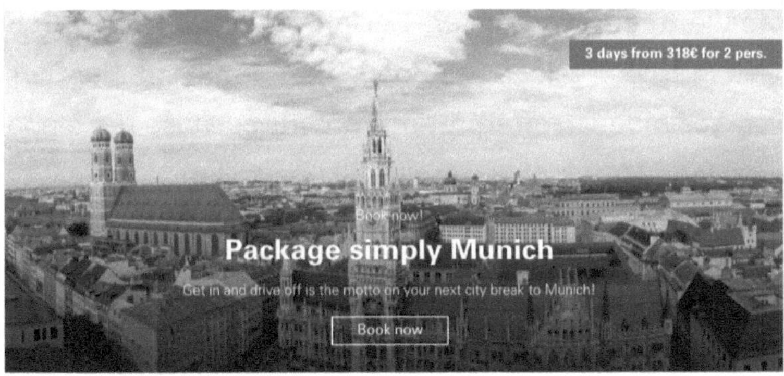

Figure 2 The Simply Munich homepage (https://www.munich.travel, February 2020)

g. The seventh step: impacts and web reputation

The investments made in the implementation and maintenance of the web presence strategy and the strategy's effect on the measures adopted to address overtourism problems should also be evaluated in the light of the results achieved. An initial evaluation could be based on the "popularity" indices (see the web presence matrix for some examples), and on navigation data, which organizations can monitor using tools of varying sophistication. Simply Munich could use the services offered by alexa.com for example, which identifies competing sites and provides data on users, on key words used for searches, on potentially useful keywords for increasing the site's viewers, etc. More generally, this step involves monitoring the impact of the tourism board activities and the Web provides a very useful "environment" in which to do this. Indeed, it is possible to search and analyse everything posted online about a particular subject in order first to ascertain sentiment and, secondly – through more detailed content analysis – to track web reputation, to make changes both online, on the web, and, most importantly, to real world services. Regarding Munich, for example, tools like Rankur, Social Mention or Social Searcher, [34] when the free versions are applied, and making allowances for the mistakes made in interpreting content because the elaboration of natural language in those tools still has its limits, reveal that the sentiment about the city is positive. However, a not inconsiderable number of negative comments also appear; as regards the

---

[34] rankur.com, socialmention.com, social-searcher.com

Oktoberfest, most of the negative content consists of comments or photos posted about similar events organized all over the world; the criticisms of the Oktoberfest refer to issues around the presence of children (a babysitting service could be organized to improve the quality of the many events and services for families); noise; and overcrowding (including in the city's beer halls). To help cope with the latter, more data could be gathered by sensor networks. This would, for example, serve to refine the performance of the Oktoberfest Barometer which currently gives information about crowding at the festival based only on a threefold division of the day.

An extremely useful conceptual tool for planning and implementing web presence strategies for tourist destinations is the model proposed by Laudon K.C. and Laudon J.P. (2020) It allows us to summarize the most important information and decisions about the steps of the method proposed above. The fact that information systems have a modular structure means that the model can be applied, like in the example of Simply Munich, also to support the design of web presence strategies, exploiting IoT devices, and even, eventually, cyber-physical systems.

Their model Laudon and Laudon model can function as a starting point for a design in which, through the appropriate use of information systems and the 7Loci method (Fig. 3), a web presence that supports chosen strategies for dealing with (or preventing) problems associated with overtourism can be created.

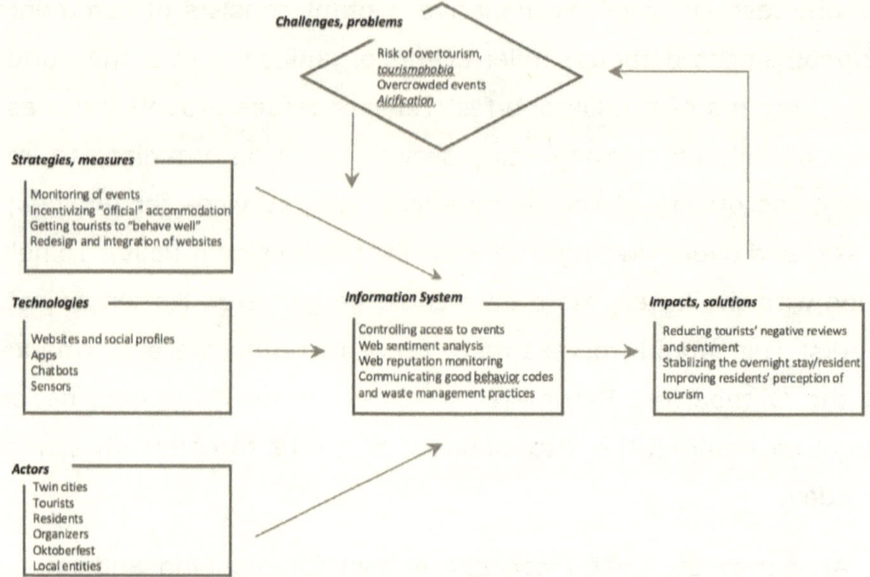

Figure 3. The information systems approach and the 7Loci method: addressing overtourism in Munich

In conclusion, although on the one hand Munich risks causing or exacerbating the problems of overtourism, on the other, its communications policies and strategies represent good practice. One positive example is the involvement of bloggers who describe their stays in the city, highlighting the authenticity of their lived experience. Others include the suggested "visit plans/programs" for stays of different duration and the excellent navigation menu.

4.6 Conclusions

Recent years have seen the rapid expansion of technologies and IT solutions applicable to tourist flows management, revealing new opportunities for halting or at least mitigating the problems linked to overtourism in the perspective of a digital tourism ecosystem. The speed at which technologies are evolving opens spaces for creative solutions, some as yet unexplored but potentially very useful. On the other hand, the importance of digital technologies for combatting overtourism must not be overestimated; overtourism is a social phenomenon, in which citizens, residents and tourists find themselves "competing" for space. And, indeed, technology is also to blame for some of the problems of overtourism (as in the case of platforms like Airbnb).

A wide range of strategies is available for tourist flow management: since no strategy or measure is suited to all contexts, choosing which to adopt and how to implement it a though challenge, the success of which depends on a proper analysis of a destination's particular problems, the design choices made and, of course, the collaboration of those involved. Information systems theory therefore points towards an approach in which the necessary first step is an analysis of the overtourism phenomena specific to the destination in question. Based on this analysis, the most appropriate technologies for supporting the measures chosen to manage tourist flows can be identified and applied.

Since the Web plays an important part in flow management systems, a digital tourism ecosystem requires an effective web presence. The 7Loci method provides a structured method and process for doing this, and models for illustrating the strategies, monitoring their outcomes and planning improvements.

Bibliography

DELLA LUCIA, M., ZENI, N., MICH, L. & FRANCH, M. (2010). Assessing the economic impact of cultural events: a methodology based on applying action-tracking technologies. *Information Technology & Tourism, 12*(3), 249-267, https://doi.org/10.3727/109830511X12978702284435

FRITH, J. (2019). *A Billion Little Pieces: RFID and Infrastructures of Identification,* MITP.

GREGORINI, B., LUCESOLI, M., BERNARDINI, G., QUAGLIARINI, E. & D'ORAZIO, M. (2020). Combining Conservation and Visitors' Fruition for Sustainable Building Heritage Use: Application to a Hypogeum. In Littlewood J., Howlett R., Capozzoli A., Jain L. (eds) Sustainability in Energy and Buildings. Smart Innovation. *Systems and Technologies, 163,* Springer, Singapore.

LAOUDIAS, C., MOREIRA, A., KIM, S., LEE, S., WIROLA, L. & FISCHIONE, C. (2018). A Survey of Enabling Technologies for Network Localization, Tracking, and Navigation. *IEEE Communications Surveys & Tutorials, 20*(4), 3607-3644, https://doi.org/10.1109/COMST.2018.2855063

LAUDON, K. C. & LAUDON, J. P. (2020). *Management Information Systems: Managing the Digital Firm,* 16th Edition, Pearson.

LOWE, D. (1999). Web engineering or web gardening, *WebNet Journal, 1*(1), 9-10.

MICH, L. (2017). Destination marketing and web presence strategies. In *Management and marketing of tourim destinations* (in Italian) McGraw Hill, Milan, 277-335.

MICH, L., KIYAVITSKAYA, N. (2011). Mapping the Web Presences of Tourism Destinations: An Analysis of the European Countries. In: Law R., Fuchs M., Ricci F. (eds) *Information and Communication Technologies in Tourism*, Springer, Vienna, https://doi.org/10.1007/978-3-7091-0503-0_31

MICH, L., BAGGIO, R. (2015). Evaluating Facebook pages for small hotels: a systematic approach. *Information Technology & Tourism, 15*(3), 209-231.

MILANO, C., NOVELLI, M. & CHEE,R J. M. (2019). Overtourism and Tourismphobia: A Journey Through Four Decades of Tourism Development, Planning and Local Concerns. *Tourism Planning & Development, 16*(4), 353-357, https://doi.org/10.1080/21568316.2019.1599604

NAMBERGER, P., JACKISCH, S., SCHMUDE, J. & KARL, M. (2019). Overcrowding, Overtourism and Local Level Disturbance: How Much can Munich Handle?. *Tourism Planning & Development, 16*(4), 452-472. https://doi.org/110.1080/21568316.2019.1595706

SHARPLES, M., ARISTEIDOU, M., VILLASCLARAS-FERNÁNDEZ, EL., HERODOTOU, C. & SCANLON, E. (2017). The Sense-it App: A Smartphone Toolkit for Citizen Inquiry Learning. *International Journal of Mobile and Blended Learning, 9*(2) 16–38, http://oro.open.ac.uk/view/person/ma8872.html

SHOVAL, N., SCHVIMER, Y. & TAMIR, M. (2018). Real-Time Measurement of Tourists' Objective and Subjective Emotions in Time and Space. *Journal of Travel Research, 57*(1), 3–16, https://doi.org/10.1177/0047287517691155

SHOVAL, N. (2018). *Tourism and Urban Planning in European Cities*, Routledge.

TRAN, N. K., SHENG, Q. Z., BABAR, M. A., YAO, L., ZHANG, W. E. & DUSTDAR, S. (2019). Internet of things search engine. *Communication of ACM, 62*(7), 66–73, https://doi.org/10.1145/3284763

WORLD TOURISM ORGANIZATION (UNWTO) (2018). *'Overtourism'? Understanding and Managing Urban Tourism Growth beyond Perceptions. Volume 2: Case Studies*, UNWTO, Madrid: https://www.e-unwto.org/doi/pdf/10.18111/9789284420629

Chapter 5 - Handling overtourism

Antonio Pezzano - https://www.linkedin.com/in/apezzano

5.1 Introduction

Overtourism is not only a catchphrase (buzzword), but also a brand. The term has in fact become synonymous with (any) negative consequence resulting from the growth of tourist flows. This chapter argues that the marked increase in tourist movement is not in itself problematic. Starting from the assumption that one cannot restrict the freedom of movement of people who decide to depart from their places of origin, we ask from the point of view of a professional who contributes to the search for solutions, what are the problems for a tourism destination, what are their determinants, and what tools are available to the authorities to balance the benefits and costs resulting from the increase in tourist flows. To answer these questions, the analysis is deliberately limited to solutions already practiced and studies commissioned by those who must consider feasible solutions. This approach, in addition to limiting the scope of inquiry, has the merit of considering papers that, unlike pure academic studies, ask from the outset what the real dimensions of the problems are and the feasibility of solutions to solve them. The goal is to provide those who intend to investigate the topic of overtourism for study or profession with insights that consider the physical, political, economic, and technical contexts that condition the search for solutions.

5.2 The negative impacts of increased tourist flows

The starting point for the arguments proposed in this chapter is a review of more recurrent types of negative impacts attributed to increased tourist flows (Table 1) reflecting three sources: the first is the list of impacts identified by Peeters et al. (2018) based on 41 cases, the second is a collection of articles published online collected by the author during 2018 and 2019, and the third is documentation of plans, resolutions, or ordinances pledged by authorities in Amsterdam, Barcelona, the Cinque Terre municipalities, and Venice.

Table 1. Types of impacts attributable to overtourism

TYPE OF IMPACT	CAUSE	WHEN
risk to people's safety and security	density of attendance at circumscribed places	few days of the year corresponding with holidays and major events
infrastructure saturation	density of attendance at circumscribed places	from some days to certain times of the year
degradation tourist experience	density of attendance at circumscribed places perception of crowding	from some days to certain times of the year
erosion of tourism capital	density of attendance at circumscribed places	manifests itself from a level of a certain level of development
quality of life of residents	density of attendance at circumscribed places destination success	from some periods to year-round

5.2.1 Symptoms and types of impact of overtourism

Security risk can be declined into two sub-types. The first is determined by the density of people present in a certain place; in this case, the safety of people is put in relation to **crowd risk (or throng risk),** the difficulties of first responders, and incidents of petty crime recorded near stops and queues at monuments or public transportation nodal points. This type of impact is not among those emphasized by the media and academic research that has addressed overtourism. Most likely because it is a common risk in all situations where there are large assemblages of people such as at large sporting events and live performances. However, for authorities governing tourism destinations, it is a source of concern and, in some cases, the only area where concrete steps have been taken to mitigate it. The second type, which can be defined as ***degradation of (perceived) safety,*** manifests itself in the form of increased crime, violence and problems related to uncivilized behaviour, alcohol consumption, prostitution, gambling, and drug trafficking. In this case, the determinant would not be so much density per se, but increased tourist flows to a destination that brings with it new social and economic dynamics.

The most frequent types of impacts have to do with the carrying capacity of the sub-systems that make up a tourism destination. First, the most obvious pressure is on the infrastructure of public services. Impacts come in the form of a) dirtiness due to the difficulty of removing waste with adequate time and means; b) dirty seas and lakes because sewage treatment plants are inadequate to handle peak usage; c) lack of water at certain times of the year; and d) long waiting times and inconveniences at stations, stops, and means of public transportation services. These are inconveniences that both residents and guests of the tourism destination incur.

Hospitality services are also put under pressure. The most obvious symptoms are long queues to access tourist sites, restricted times with which to visit museums and monuments, waiting times at restaurants, soaring prices, lack of staff courtesy, and widespread noise and loutishness. The combination of these problems can result in the degradation of the tourist experience and, as a consequence, to lower levels of tourist satisfaction.

Continuing with the analysis of sub-systems with limited carrying capacity, it is the case to highlight the consumption of so-called *tourism capital*. We refer not only to the more tangible aspects, such as physical damage and erosion to monuments, cultural sites, trails, landscape pollution, etc., but also to intangible phenomena that mature over time and have, potentially, an extremely negative impact on the tourism destination. The reference is to the loss of identity of places, the so-called *gentrification of historic centres*, the homogenization of traditions, and, above all, the deterioration of the tourist image.

The last type of impact, and the most complex to analyse, is the degradation of residents' quality of life. The negative impacts of tourism on residents manifest themselves in several ways. First, the residents of a tourism destination, to the extent that they share the same spaces with tourists, suffer their own inconveniences. In addition, there are other problems not caused by tourist density, but by the development of tourism itself. The most notorious episodes are the lack of rental housing resulting in soaring prices, the disappearance of businesses and services for residents, and the increase in fees for the operation of public services.

5.2.2 An attempt to circumscribe the causes of overtourism

The first relevant finding to emerge from this review is that overtourism primarily has to do with episodes of congestion or, to be more precise, the density of attendance at specific places, at specific times of the year and times of day. *Visitor attendance density* refers to the number of people who, for reasons other than work, are in a limited space during a certain time frame. Thus, the attendance density of a space is a dynamic concept considering that the number of visitors varies over time and that the same space, in some cases, can be *changed* (think of the beneficial effect on the degree of crowding of a bus stop generated by the increase in the frequency of public transport rides).

This approach has the merit of shedding light on one point. Most analyses based on traditional tourism density indicators are inadequate both in terms of preventive analysis of the problem and as a management tool. Tourist density is given by the ratio of tourist movement to the area that hosts it. The most common indicators use the number of overnight stays by tourists as the numerator and the land area or number of inhabitants as the denominator. Even if statistical survey systems can provide accurate and reliable estimates of the number of overnight stays, tourism density indicators do not consider excursionists. Moreover, in most cases the indicators use areas and population levels attributable to administrative units (always municipal) much larger than those frequented for leisure by tourists and excursionists in the denominator. Finally, the figure is reported as one assuming a homogeneous distribution of tourist movement over the 365 days of a year. In sum, traditional tourism density indicators are not suitable for capturing the magnitude and spatial-temporal variability of the overtourism phenomenon.

The second reason that explains overtourism is the perception of crowding. While congestion (i.e., a high density of attendance at a certain place) is an objective phenomenon, crowding can be defined as a psychological response to congestion. Stokols (1972) is the first scholar, followed by many others, to qualify the psychological response as negative. Choi, Mirjafari and Weaver (1976) disagree with Stokols' hypothesis. They propose an alternative view in which the perception of crowding, and thus the negative or positive response to it, depends not only on objective phenomena (such as the level of density and behaviours), but also on the cultural and motivational codes by which these phenomena are interpreted. While Stokols' conceptualization has received much attention in, among other things, leisure studies, Choi et al.'s approach has been neglected in contemporary tourism research. This has had important consequences for the construction of crowding theory, where its inherently negative connotation has led it to be linked to the broader concepts of carrying capacity and sustainability. The theory that crowding negatively affects the degree of tourist satisfaction is thus all to be proven. Reinforcing this thesis is data provided by the Barcelona Tourism Observatory (2019) according to which the level of tourist satisfaction is high and shows signs of growth since 2014. Moreover, only half of the respondents perceive Barcelona as *full* of visitors – theses supported by analysis of online reviews that see Barcelona ranked fourth (and growing) in overall satisfaction in the top 10 European cities by tourist size.

The third and final determinant that would explain overtourism lies in the success of a tourism destination. The concept of success is qualified not so much and not only by the increase in the number of visitors, but by the change in the economic and social fabric that occurs in tourist places. In other words, tourist demand is not merely supplementing the turnover of existing businesses but is such that business establishments specifically geared toward it are springing up. This development would be such that local entrepreneurs would be pushed to invest only in tourist-oriented businesses and disinvest in those aimed at locals. Airbnb and, in general, short-term rental brokerage platforms, are accused of reproducing the same pattern in the housing market by taking away housing for residential use and increasing housing and rental prices. The latter situation has become in the news narrated by the media one of the most obvious impacts of overtourism.

The impact of Airbnb (and other real estate brokerage platforms for short rentals) is hotly debated[35]. A study focusing on the U.S. market showed that Airbnb takes houses and apartments away from residential rentals and contributes to rising prices (Barron et al., 2018). However, attributing cities' housing policy woes to increased tourist flows alone is misleading. Rising house prices

---

[35] In 2019 alone, there are dozens of articles on the topic. Among the most interesting and informed are one by Aleksandra Wisniewska that appeared on September 5, 2019 on the FinancialTimes website (*Are Airbnb investors destroying Europe's cultural capitals?*) and one by Clara Guibourg and Kevin Peachey that appeared on the BBC website on April 25, 2019 (*What the Airbnb surge means for UK cities*). In addition, the website http://insideairbnb.com provides constantly updated data, studies and research on the topic and in general on the relationship between Airbnb, neighborhoods and cities.

such as rents are not unique to tourism destinations but to all cities where there is some economic dynamism in terms of attracting investment, talent, and economic growth. In some cities, such as Amsterdam, Barcelona, Milan and Paris, general economic dynamism and tourism development go hand in hand. Other cities, such as Venice, on the other hand, are characterized by the so-called *tourism monoculture.* The question in these cases is to what extent this dependence can be attributed to the success of tourism (which displaces other investments) or to the fact that there are no alternatives to the tourist economy at a certain point in history. Finally, a general question remains in the background: to what extent then are the transformations of a city to be read negatively, when historically cities have always experienced processes of transformation?

In summary, this chapter focuses on analysing solutions to tourist congestion problems.

5.3 The solutions to the problems of attendance density of tourist places

As of 2017, major institutions have produced studies and research reports in which they propose solutions to overtourism, including those specifically aimed at managing problems arising from congestion[36]. None of these papers report a solution whose

---

[36] The studies promoted by the Travel and Tourism Industry Forum (WTTC and McKinsey&Company, 2017), the European Parliament (Peeters et al., 2018) and the World Tourism Organization (UNWTO, 2018) were consulted in writing this chapter.

effectiveness has been assessed with empirical evidence in open or semi-closed systems such as a city, neighbourhood or village. One must therefore be aware that we are still in an experimental phase and that evaluations are made based on logical rather than factual evidence.

Among the most widely used and effective measures, at least on a logical level, is increasing capacity. Typically, action is taken to increase the supply of basic services such as security, municipal solid waste collection, and public transportation. Action is taken both in terms of infrastructure (but it takes a long time) and in terms of service (e.g., increased staffing, increased vehicles, etc.). The essential trait of these measures is that they are organized to manage seasonal peaks while causing extra costs to local communities, which in many cases do not have the analytical tools to identify them (Epler Wood et al., 2019).

5.3.1 Measures to influence visitor behaviour

A common strategy to mitigate the effects of overtourism is to act on visitor behaviours. In this sense, one does not question the level of congestion per se, but seeks to curb the behaviours (of visitors) that are deemed most socially troublesome or have the potential to cause harm to people or property. At least half of the cases surveyed by Peeters et al. (2018) consist of public order measures. In Italy, these measures can be traced back to the ordinances by which mayors prepare orders and bans at certain times of the year (or permanently in cities) for sites of high cultural or environmental value and for places of high attendance. A second type of measures concerns communication campaigns such as #EnjoyRespectVenice promoted to orient visitors toward adopting a responsible behaviour that respects the environment, landscape, artistic beauty and identity of Venice and its inhabitants. The goal of these campaigns is to raise awareness of the impact of tourism and spread a responsible way of traveling.

Finally, a measure often invoked as a structural solution, but difficult to implement, is to rethink the mix of products offered and attract so-called quality tourism. To understand the issue well, consider the case of Megaluf, the resort on the island of Majorca (in the Balearic Islands) known for its unbridled nightlife, whose events have found their way into crime news. The most serious episodes involve balconing, the fashion of throwing oneself from hotel balconies in an attempt to hit the water of the hotel pool. A practice that has unfortunately resulted in deaths and injuries. Another fundamental problem is the contagion of diseases due to the frequency with which unprotected casual sex occurs. The city is persistently trying to renew its image and attract tourist flows other than the traditional British youth. Since 2012, Meliá Hotels International, one of the largest hotel chains in the area, has been working on a long-term plan to transform the negative perception of the destination. Seven years later, and after investments of hundreds of millions of euros, Magaluf is one of the most buzzed-about resorts in Spain. Thanks to the ripple effect on the rest of the industry, nearly 70 percent of hotel beds in Magaluf are now in 4- and 5-star hotels, well above the average for both Mallorca and Spain. It is still too early to say whether the image of Megaluf, or the tourist flows have changed. However, two useful lessons can be drawn for those who intend to embark on a similar path. The first is that one must be clear about what is meant by quality tourism. It is a generic statement that needs to be qualified by thinking about precise demand targets. The second lesson is that it often takes substantial investment, especially private investment, to create new products and services for the identified target audience.

5.3.2 The measures of dispersion of flows in space

These are the measures intended to encourage visitation to secondary locations or less-travelled routes. Their political appeal is so obvious that they are sometimes referred to as measures to "redistribute" flows. A distinction should be made between measures that promote alternative tourist places and sites with the ambition of enriching supply and those that expressly aim to replace visits to popular destinations and sites with lesser-known ones. In the former case, the measure of success is the fact that in addition to famous place X, places Y and Z were also visited. In this situation, the impact on attendance density would result from a shorter stay (in terms of hours or days) at the most famous site or destination. In the second case, success can be measured by the consolidation or decrease in tourist flow to X, in favour of places Y and Z. Unfortunately, even though these measures are all the rage in both policy announcements and planning documents, there are few cases of actual implementation and no evidence of their usefulness.

The reasons for the inadequacy of these measures are obvious. First, stated or adopted strategies rely on greater public investment in marketing lesser-known places. Unfortunately, the effectiveness of tourism destination marketing is often overstated.

In addition, little attention is paid to assessing the appropriateness of the size and quality of investments needed to produce certain effects. One cannot expect to change established patterns of tourist behaviour with small (and one-time) investments entrusted to small organizations that often lack adequate capacity and experience. And this brings us to the second reason for inadequacy: tourist behaviour.

Tourist destinations reported in overtourism maps have at least one common characteristic: most visitors are excursionists or first (or second) time visitors. These two types of visitors have remarkably similar behaviours: they walk long distances and (in large cities) frequently use the public transportation system to reach major tourist attractions. For this type of visitor, a successful visit can be achieved by following a dense schedule that requires efficient planning and physical endurance. Consequently, their urban mobility patterns can be predicted: First, a heavy concentration at the most popular sites and on the streets that connect these places, and second, a very superficial visit of both places and major attractions. These behavioural patterns have been confirmed by many empirical observations (Frytag, 2010; Mckercher and Lau, 2008; Shoval and Isaacson, 2007).

Amsterdam is probably the city that has focused the most on dispersal strategies. The first attempts date back to 2001. Recently, solutions pioneered in Amsterdam have been reported in the media and policy documents mentioned earlier. In 2016, the Visit Amsterdam team developed an app (called Discover the City) that alerts users when an attraction is busy and, more importantly, suggests alternatives. The app is no longer available for download, and other ongoing experiments have not yet yielded the desired results. An especially useful analysis in this regard is provided by Dirk Kloosterboer, author of the blog dirkmjk.nl, specializing in georeferenced data. In a very well-argued and data-driven post[37] he has shown that after 20 years, while it is true that there are new stops on city tours, 75 percent of the places to visit listed by Lonely Planet are in the centre of the city.

5.3.3 Measures of flow dispersion over time

Measures of flow dispersion over time assume that a place has a certain carrying capacity that is exceeded (even abundantly) during some peak periods, but is under control during the rest of the year. Efficient management of space over time, i.e., shifting visitor flows from peak to off-peak periods, theoretically allows influx to be limited within load limits, and thus safeguard the balance of a destination's physical, social, and economic components. These kinds of practices are already in use in closed systems and are based on two pillars: a) a limited number of admissions in a day or certain time slots and b) an admission reservation system. Popular examples are the reservation-based visitation systems of Machu Picchu (Peru) and that of Park Güell (Barcelona), both UNESCO sites. In Italy, the reservation (or regulated access) system, popularized in the media as *a numero chiuso* (closed number), is in

---

[37] https://dirkmjk.nl/en/113/is-tourist-dispersion-working-an-analysis-of-lonely-planet-maps

place at some trails and valleys in protected areas and, for the past few years, at some particularly valuable beaches[38].

At present, there are no practices for managing and contingency of tourist flows in semi-open systems and thus in small or large cities or in some circumscribed areas of the cities themselves. However, the Venice City Council, during 2019, adopted a series of actions that will lead the city to have a complex reservation system for entrances to the ancient city by 2023. For this reason, Venice, and specifically the studies, proposals and experiments that have taken place over the past twenty years, are an indispensable laboratory for understanding the opportunities, constraints, and risks of policies for managing tourist flows[39]. As of now, it is therefore only possible to highlight what are the nodes to be considered in designing a system of dispersion of tourist flows over time.

The first node is to understand that tourism destination is not a stable and unambiguous concept, but a dynamic and variable one. Therefore, the administrative boundaries by which we are

---

[38] In the Adamello Brenta Nature Park, regulated access is provided in summer in Val di Genova (2013), Val di Tovel, Vallesinella, Ritort, Val di Fumo, and Val d'Algone. Since 2018, access is also regulated at Lake Braies in Val Pusteria. In Sardinia, regulated access is provided at the beaches of Tuerredda, in the southwestern part of the island; there are also the beaches of Cala Biriola, Cala Goloritzé, and Cala Mariolu, and further south the beach of Punta Molentis in Villasimius. There are guided tours but limited number in the Tuscan archipelago si Pianosa and Montecristo.

[39] The COSES 141.0 report (2009), Venice Project Center report (2014), Venice Tourism Territorial Governance Project (2017), Venice City Council Resolutions Nos. 69 and 109, the official newsletter of the City of Venice were consulted for the preparation of this chapter.

accustomed to thinking are misleading. For tourists, the destination changes depending on the type of trip and the place of origin. For example, Cinque Terre is one of the most advertised (and sold) trips as a one-day tour from Florence. Venice itself is recommended-given the excessive cost of overnight stays-as a day trip from Florence, Milan, Verona, Bologna, and other cities in northern Italy. For many tourists from the American continent or Asia, the trip to Italy is an itinerary (sometimes within a larger European itinerary) where stops, things to see, times of stay, and places to stay overnight are decided primarily in consideration of budget and logistical constraints. The so-called day-tripper tourism, that is, the stay of a few days or – increasingly frequent – a few hours in popular tourism destinations such as Venice, the Cinque Terre or the Amalfi Coast is the consequence of a few converging phenomena. Apart from the explosion of low-cost flights, which has favoured weekend stays in the cities, one must consider the behaviour of tourist flows from emerging countries and in general from non-European countries. For many of these tourists, Italy is one of the must-see places where one must go at least once in a lifetime, even if only for a few hours. The ease of travel between Italian cities – especially in Central Italy – in terms of options, comfort, and speed of means of transportation, favours this mode of tourist enjoyment of the *Bel Paese*.

Therefore, for those who must plan and manage tourism flows, it is appropriate to think in terms of a micro-destination or network. A micro-destination is defined, as proposed by Hernadez-Martin et al. (2016), as a well-defined geographic space (even within a municipality) and characterized by intense tourist activity, certain patterns of tourist behaviour, and a specific tourist image.

The micro-destination therefore can be the historical centre of a city, a neighbourhood, a square, an attraction or a set of small municipalities. Beritelli et al. (2015) propose to read the destination as the set of itineraries traced by visitors that always have a pivot (system head) determining them. Complex realities such as Amsterdam, Barcelona, and Venice, analysed from this perspective, offer interesting insights, and can lead – as in the case of Barcelona – to conclusions different from those emphasized by the media. It is not the whole city that suffers some problems, but a well-delimited part of it.

It is worth considering that analyses of phenomena and intervention areas may have varying structures. For example, in Venice the area subject to analyses of urban sustainability and carrying capacity models is the ancient city, while the area subject to regulated access could be the Marciana Area alone (that part of urban space between St. Mark's Square, the Procuratie, the Piazzetta dei Leoncini, and the pier between the Ponte della Paglia and the Ponte dell'Accademia dei Pittori). This is because legal constraints (constitutional right to freedom of movement) and technical, economic, and political assessments must be considered when designing and implementing such systems.

The second crucial point to consider is how to set the maximum number of visitors that can be admitted to the regulated access of the micro-destination. Its value depends on a complex interaction between several variables, such as the morphological characteristics of spaces, the expectations of visitors, residents and tourist entrepreneurs, and the seasonality of flows. The interaction of these variables is dynamic and changes over time; therefore, it is not useful and advisable to determine a unique fixed value (Iorio and Sistu, 2002). For this reason, the important COSES (2009) study for Venice (Consortium for Research and Training), cautions against a single number and suggests a calculation methodology that dynamically considers not only structural variables (e.g., steamboat service or rubbish collection service may be incremented in the face of certain peaks), but also policy preferences[40] and actual flow management capacity. When machine learning was not yet fashionable, COSES recommended using Venice's capacity study method as a starting point. By envisioning its use through a computer platform, it was expected that

> "As the management information platform increases its memory (that which happened and was detected, user-generated content), will increase the ability to simulate saturation forecasts, contingent upon (if anything) probability-based projections." (Sustainable Tourism in Venice, 2009, p. 6)

In assessing the carrying capacity of a destination, it is necessary to consider that it is composed of subsystems (e.g., accommodation, public establishments, museums, public transportation, squares, streets, etc.). Each of them has its own degree of saturation that potentially contributes to defining the carrying capacity of the entire destination. Knowing the degree of saturation in time is relatively easy for sub-systems subject to reservation (e.g.,

---

[40] For example, to whom to give priority. To only tourists staying overnight in the ancient city, or also to those staying overnight in the four municipalities of the *Venetian mainland*? How to consider the excursionists? All equally or differentiate between those staying overnight in the province of Venice and other provinces in the Veneto region?

parking spaces at parking lots, transportation, museum visits, etc.), but it is very difficult for many urban spaces, such as the pedestrian capacity of squares and streets, and in any case, it is rather complicated for the network of urban factors themselves (blocking one access, choosing an alternative access). Therefore, it becomes necessary not only to provide monitoring systems for urban components (feasible today with low investment) but to have a single collection system for these data. This is a working hypothesis that is actually difficult to implement and that becomes overly complex as the geographic area and the institutions involved in land management expand.

This observation highlights another node: the coordination of regulated-access management systems in tourism destinations. Take for example a destination such as the Cinque Terre. Trenitalia, the carrier that provides the most widely used mode of transportation to arrive in and transit through the area, has a Service Agreement with the Region of Liguria that runs from 2018 to 2032; however, the agreement does not provide for forms of coordination with municipalities[41]. Cruise passengers, a large component of visitors, arrive from three ports (Genoa, Livorno, and La Spezia) managed by their own management authority. Access also depends on

---

[41] The contract not only fails to provide for forms of coordination for the management of tourist flows, but it also secretes the data on the same flows. A ruling issued by the second section of the Regional Administrative Court for Liguria (published on Dec. 20, 2019, "orders the Region of Liguria to allow access, by viewing and extracting a copy, to Annexes No. 3 and No. 5 of the Contract for Regional and Local Public Transport Service entered into with Trenitalia for the period 2018-2032, as well as by communicating the number of Cinque Terre fare tickets sold and the related revenue".

the number of parking lots, seaports and NCCs (rental with driver); these are all subjects whose regulatory regime is managed by different authorities. With this fragmented system of authority, not only is it difficult to monitor flows, but it is impossible to plan any form of regulated access management.

Therefore, it is not a coincidence, that to date the cases for regulated access are confined to the quoted cruise ship dockings of Dubrovinik and Santorini: two measures that are still not considered sufficient to solve the peak problems of these two places.

In Italy, the only regulated access initiatives implemented, or potentially implemented, relate to managing crowding risk. Since 2018, during major tourist events, gates have been active in Venice that, upon reaching a threshold of 23,000 people in the San Marco area, close to avoid excessive overcrowding. The closure, which is temporary, is limited to the time it takes for the density level in the area to drop below the expected threshold values. The experiments conducted in 2018 and 2019 were successful – according to comments found in the press – partly due to the widespread presence of specially trained personnel to manage the flows and the gates themselves.

In Riomaggiore (Cinque Terre), the municipal administration, as part of the civil protection plan, has prepared a plan to cope with the risk of crowding. Load limits of areas deemed to be at risk were then calculated and emergency measures were prepared to be implemented if these limits were exceeded. Specifically, the mayor of Riomaggiore adopted an ordinance (Number 7, dated 4/13/2019) assuming the authority to impose on Trenitalia (carrier) and RFI, Reti Ferroviarie Italiane (manager of the railway infrastructure), the maximum limit of people who can stand in the stations of Riomaggiore and Manarola, among the most densely crowded points in the entire area. Trenitalia and RFI appealed against this ordinance, and the Regional Administrative Tribunal (TAR) for Liguria issued a ruling (published on 06/26/19) that recognized the mayor's reasons, but upheld Trenitalia and RFI's appeal because the ordinance constitutes "vague prescriptions lacking concretely preceptive content." Most interestingly, the TAR recognizes that rights and freedom of movement can be balanced against security reasons. In the ruling it is written that "the Cinque Terre as a whole, and Riomaggiore and Manarola specifically, have a railway infrastructure and access to it that inevitably "pays the price" for the very characteristics of these places, which, if, on the one hand, undoubtedly constitute a reason for fascination and a tourist attraction, on the other hand, pose problems of compatibility with a market that is expanding and must, therefore, necessarily be regulated."

5.4 Conclusions

Reading the research papers, journal articles, policy documents and measures consulted, leads to the conclusion that overtourism is seen as the source of many problems, sometimes without the necessary insights. To deal with it, authorities act by resorting to the traditional bureaucratic tools of command and control. The outcomes of some measures are unclear; others are logically fallacious.

Increased tourist flows are not a problem per se, but an economic opportunity, and should be managed as such. It should be acknowledged that the invasion of visitors brings inconvenience to a part of the cities' population that deserves compensation. If there is a scarce resource (urban space), it cannot be made freely available, or everyone will try to use it at the same time (congestion), leading to unsatisfactory results for everyone. Therefore, the solution is to introduce a kind of congestion charge, a mechanism that has proven effective in decreasing car traffic, the pollution it generates, and promoting alternative forms of transportation to the car.

The establishment of the congestion charge (or entrance fee) presents itself as a textbook case: faced with the growing negative externalities (on residents and tourist capital) generated by an increasing flow of visitors, action is taken to internalize them on those who generate them. From a practical point of view, entrance fee's effectiveness depends on a number of factors that can be considered in the design and management phase. While many cities have considered introducing it, there are only a few success stories. What do they have in common? In this sense, the lessons learned from the introduction of the congestion charge for automobile traffic are a useful source of inspiration.

The entrance fee for urban centres with high tourist demand is effective (for decongestion purposes) only if there is a quota on flows (closed number). Since a sizeable proportion of tourist demand is inelastic with respect to price, there would be benefits to municipal funds, but flows would remain unchanged. A textbook case is the increase in ticket cost (for tourists) of the vaporetto in Venice, which has not changed the frequency and intensity of its use. The introduction of the disembarkation fee in Venice, which is expected to take effect from January 16, 2023, goes in the same direction. Paying a sum of up to ten euros on the highest congestion days will not be a deterrent to those from the other side of the world.

To work, an entry ticket – especially in the case of contingent tourist flows – needs strong political will and centralized management of all forms of transportation and access control to the urban centre. Constitutional and legal issues, as well as the strong need for coordination of information and tools currently under the control of different agencies, need strong political will and management to be overcome.

The design of the introduction of a ticket must necessarily be open and consider comments and requests from all stakeholders. Pervasive information (using all available means), the possibility of reporting problems, and, most importantly, the possibility of making corrections to consider stakeholders' feedback have turned out to be key ingredients. With this in mind, decisions such as the maximum number of eligible visitors, exemptions, and the possibility of introducing differential pricing based on the types of visitors, should be subjected not only to technical scrutiny but also to open discussion with stakeholders.

Finally, the introduction of a ticket must be accompanied by a program of investments that make it easier and smoother for residents and tourists to move around the urban centres where it is introduced. A program such as this could be financed by the ticket revenues themselves. However, these revenues could also be used in other ways. In this regard, an original suggestion – absent from the debate – was proposed by Carlo Lottieri in an article published in Il Foglio on August 23, 2017.

"What to do with this money? It is usually suggested that it be used for public maintenance of the city: and this is not surprising, because an increasingly *nationalized* city needs increasing amounts of resources. Only by reversing the logic and imagining that the city is handed back to its owners can one think that the proceeds of the access ticket go to families.

If these revenues were earmarked for individual Venetians each could receive a sum on the order of a thousand euros. In essence, a family of four would get an annual contribution, to compensate for the tourist invasion, of about 4,000 euros: a sum that could help stop the exodus and might even entice some Venetians who have already moved to Mestre to back off.

Of course, such a hypothesis is absent from the debate today. No one has so far assumed that it is the Venetians themselves, namely those who suffer first-hand the nuisances associated with tourist attendance, who are the beneficiaries of the entrance fee. And the reason is clear: Venice has completely lost all its vocation for free enterprise, is a prisoner of a bureaucratic mentality, and increasingly represents — except for tourism and the liberal professions — a conglomerate of various state-owned activities (health, university, region, school, etc.) which continues to invest in political logic.

Giving the proceeds of the tourist tax and the similar tax for day tourists directly to families means betting on social viability: on individuals rather than bureaucracies, on families rather than the state.

For the idea of introducing a kind of "pollution fax" that finances Venice residents to be accepted, it is, in short, necessary for the city to understand that it can only be saved by those who live it: looking at Venetians as active individuals, responsible owners, potential entrepreneurs of a true renaissance, and not already mere objects of redistributive policies, spatial plans, taxes and regulations. But will Venice be able to rediscover that adventurous spirit that once made it great? The gamble is all here.

(*The illusion that kills Venice. The city of small stores will never return. The questionable policy of prohibitions that undermines all property rights only hastens its decline.*)"

In summary, the main points in handling overtourism are as follows. Overtourism has become synonymous with the negative consequences of tourism. Increased tourist flows can generate congestion problems in tourism destinations. Often these situations are circumscribed in space and time, but nevertheless, in theory, they can negatively affect the lives of residents and tourists themselves, even to the point of leading to the erosion of the tourism capital on which a destination's economic activity is based. In practice, although there are borderline cases; empirical evidence shows that many of the reported problems can be solved with better management of urban policies. At present, the policies and tools used consider legal, political, and organizational constraints more than actual visitor behaviour. Therefore, they are doomed to failure. However, the positive outcomes of introducing *congestion charges* in some cities as a tool to limit vehicular traffic offer interesting food for thought. Tourism growth is primarily an economic opportunity. From this point of view, tourism congestion is an inconvenience for the residents of the affected areas. For this reason, they must be compensated, with a monetary transfer from tourists to them. How these transfers are designed, how they are managed and, most importantly, how the resources received are used, will increasingly determine the fate of *overtourist* destinations in the future.

Bibliography

AIROLDI, A. & CINI, T. (2014). Access to metropolitan areas. Areas of intervention and prospects for solutions, (in Italian) https://www.unibocconi.it/wps/wcm/connect/c046c202-9991-4edb-860a-55e6852f44b2/ASPI_Report_2014.pdf?MOD=AJPERES

BARRON, K., KUNG, E. & PROSERPIO, D. (2018). The Effect of Home-Sharing on House Prices and Rents: Evidence from Airbnb, https://ssrn.com/abstract=3006832

BERITELLI, P., REINHOLD, S., LAESSER, C. & BIEGER, T. (2015). The St. Gallen Model for Destination Management.

BIVENS, G. (2019). The economic costs and benefits of Airbnb. No reason for local policymakers to let Airbnb bypass tax or regulatory obligations. *Report of the Economic Policy Institute*, https://www.epi.org/publication/the-economic-costs-and-benefits-of-airbnb-no-reason-for-local-policymakers-to-let-airbnb-bypass-tax-or-regulatory-obligations

CHOI, S. C., MIRJAFARI, A. & WEAVER, H. B. (1976). The Concept of Crowding: A Critical Review and Proposal of an Alternative Approach. *Environment and Behaviour*, *8*, 345-362.

COSES (2009). Rapporto 141.0. *Turismo sostenibile a Venezia.* Studio per il Coordinamento delle Strategie Turistiche del Comune di Venezia.

EPLER WOOD, M., MILSTEIN, M. & AHAMED-BROADHURST, K. (2019). *Destinations at Risk*: *The Invisible Burden of Tourism*. The Travel Foundation.

FREYTAG, T. (2010), *Déjàvu: Tourist practices of repeat visitors in the city of Paris*. Social Geography (SG). 5. 10.5194/sg-5-49-2010.

HERNÁNDEZ-MARTÍN, R., SIMANCAS-CRUZ, M. R., GONZÁLEZ-YANES, J. A., RODRÍGUEZ-RODRÍGUEZ, Y., GARCÍA-CRUZ, J. I & GONZÁLEZ-MORA, Y. M. (2016). Identifying micro-destinations and providing statistical information: a pilot study in the Canary Islands, *Current Issues in Tourism*, *19*(8), 771-790.

IORIO, M. & SISTU, G. (2002). Sviluppo turistico e capacità di carico ambientale in Sardegna. IN PACI R., USAI S. (Eds.), L'ULTIMA SPIAGGIA, CUEC, CAGLIARI, ISBN 88-8467-065-9, PP. 241-280.

MCKERCHER, B. & LAU, G. (2010). Movement patterns of tourists within a destination. *Tour. Geogr.*, *10*, 355–374.

OBSERBATORI DEL TURUSME A BARCELONA) (2019). *Monitor de reputació turística online de Ciutat Barcelona*, 2018.

OBSERBATORI DEL TURUSME A BARCELONA (2019). *Perfil i hàbits dels turistes a la Ciutat de Barcelona*, 2018.

PEETERS, P., GÖSSLING, S., KLIJS, J., MILANO, C., NOVELLI, M., DIJKMANS, C., EIJGELAAR, E., HARTMAN, S., HESLINGA, J., ISAAC, R., MITAS, O., MORETTI, S., NAWIJN, J., PAPP, B. AND POSTMA, A., (2018), Research for TRAN Committee – *Overtourism: impact and possible policy responses,* European Parliament, Policy Department for Structural and Cohesion Policies, Brussels.

QIU, S., TUN, T. H., & HIDALGO, D. (2018). Toward Car-Free Cities: 3 Reasons Why London's Congestion Charge Is Working. https://thecityfix.com/blog/toward-car-free-cities-3-reasons-londons-congestion-charge-working-shiyong-qiu-thet-hein-tundario-hidalgo/?utm_source=feedburner&utm_medium=feed&utm_campaign=Feed%3A+thecityfix%2Fposts+(TheCityFix)

SHOVAL, N. & ISAACSON, M. (2007). Sequence alignment as a method for human activity analysis in space and time. *Ann. Assoc. Am. Geogr.*, *97*(2), 282–29.

SKAPINKER., M. (2015). Magaluf tests the limits of rebranding as it sobers up. *The Financial Times*, November 4, 2015.

STOKOLS, D. (1972). A Social-Psychological Model of Human Crowding Phenomena. *Journal of the American Planning Association*, *38*(2), 72-83.

VENICE PROJECT CENTER (2014). Analysing the Impacts of Tourism on the City of Venice. *An Interdisciplinary Qualifying Project Submitted to the faculty of Worcester Polytechnic Institute in partial fulfilment of the requirements for the Degree of Bachelor of Science*, https://web.wpi.edu/Pubs/E-project/Available/E-project-121914-094957/unrestricted/VE14-TOUR_FinalReport.pdf

WORLD TOURISM ORGANIZATION (UNWTO), CENTRE OF EXPERTISE LEISURE, TOURISM & HOSPITALITY, NHTV BREDA UNIVERSITY OF APPLIED SCIENCES & NHL STENDEN UNIVERSITY OF APPLIED SCIENCES (2018). *'Overtourism'? – Understanding and Managing Urban Tourism Growth beyond Perceptions,* Executive Summary, UNWTO, Madrid.

Plans, deliberations, ordinances

Amsterdam
City in Balance 2018-2022. Towards a new equilibrium between quality of life and hospitality (28.03.2019)

Barcelona
Tourism 2020 Barcelona, Strategic Plan https://ajuntament.barcelona.cat/turisme/en/strategic-plan
Special Tourist Accommodation Plan (PEUAT), https://ajuntament.barcelona.cat/pla-allotjaments-turistics/en

Riomaggiore
Piano speditivo di protezione civile del comune di Riomaggiore, https://www.comune.riomaggiore.sp.it/index.php?option=com_content&view=article&id=451&Itemid=163

Venezia
Progetto di Governance Territoriale a Venezia (2017)
Council Resolution N° 69 del 28/02/2019, Contributo di accesso alla Città Antica del Comune di Venezia e alle altre isole minori della laguna, ai sensi e per gli effetti dell'art. 1 comma 1129 della legge n. 145 del 30/12/2018 approvazione tariffe
Council Resolution N° 109 del 29/03/2019, Regolamento per l'istituzione e la disciplina del contributo di accesso, con qualsiasi vettore, alla Città Antica del Comune di Venezia e alle altre isole minori della laguna – approvazione delle modalità operative previste dagli artt. 4, 5 e 8.
https://live.comune.venezia.it/it/2019/12/la-giunta-approva-un-piano-da-10-milioni-di-euro-la-gestione-del-turismo-venezia

edizioni intra

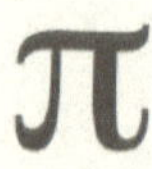

Politicamente
Saggi e scritti politici

Brĕvitĕr
Manuali e compendi giuridici

Università

Visio
Arti grafiche e visive

Teatro da leggere
Testi teatrali

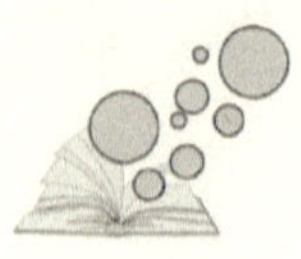

Mille bolle blu
Libri per bambini

www.intraedizioni.it